# VET SCHOOL PROFILES

## Veterinary Medical School Admissions Data and Analysis

Rachel A. Winston, Ph.D.

Lizard Publishing is not sponsored by any college. While data was derived by school, state, or nationally published sources, some statistics may be out of date as published sources vary widely based upon the date of submission and currency of numbers. Attempts were made to obtain the best information during the writing of this book from American Veterinary Medical Association, American Association of Veterinary Medical College Application Service, Veterinary Information Network, Student American Veterinary Medical Association, American Association of Equine Practitioners, World Veterinary Association, The Student Doctor Network, NCES, U.S. Census Bureau, U.S. Department of Education, Common Data Set, College Board, U.S. News & World Report, college, and other organizational sites. Descriptions of colleges are a compilation of college website information as well as student, faculty, and staff interviews with individuals and often from unique experiences and impressions. Attempts were made to triangulate multiple points of light. If you would like to share program information, data, or an impression of a specific college, please write to Lizard Publishing at the address below or at the e-mail address: *info@mylizard.org.*

ISBN  978-1946432384 (hardback);  978-1946432346 (paperback);  978-1946432391 (e-book)

LCCN: 2021920095

© Copyright 2021 Lizard Publishing. All rights reserved.

All rights reserved. No part of this work may be reproduced or transmitted in any form or by any means, including, but not limited to, photocopying, recording, image capture, electronic, mechanical or any other information storage and retrieval systems, without the express written permission from Lizard Publishing.®

Lizard Publishing® 7700 Irvine Center Drive, Suite 800 Irvine, CA 92618 *www.lizard-publishing.com*

Lizard Publishing creates, designs, produces, and distributes books and resources to provide academic, admissions, and career information. Our mental process is fueled by three tenets:

- Ignite the hunger to learn and the passion to make a difference
- Illuminate the expanse of knowledge by sharing cutting edge thinking
- Innovate to create a world that makes the transition from dreams to reality

We work with academic leaders who transform the educational landscape to publish relevant content and advise students of their educational and professional options, with the aim of developing 21st-century learners and leaders. We also work with students to publish their books and present widely diverse ideas to the college/graduate school-bound community. With headquarters in Irvine, California, Lizard Publishing works virtually with authors to edit, publish, and distribute both hard copy and paperback books.

This book was published in the U.S.A. Lizard Publishing is a premium quality provider of educational reference, career guidance, and motivational publications/merchandise for global learners, educators, and stakeholders in education.

Book design by Michelle Tahan *www.michelletahan.com*

Book formatting by Obinna Chinemerem Ozuo

LIZARD PUBLISHING

This book is dedicated to animal lovers everywhere who cannot imagine a day without animals in their lives.

This book was inspired by Charlie Banks, Michael Chian, and Gracie Hare.

Coming from a long line of Wisconsin and Illinois farmers, I appreciate the compassion, care, and disciplined work ethic of those raised on a farm. Long hours and constant attention to animal welfare and nutrition is a labor of love.

Surrounded by companion animal lovers has also provided a keen insight into the close relationship individuals have with their pets. However, I have also supported students in their quest to attend vet school and numerous students whose youth was spent with show horses, inspiring me further to understand a bigger picture of animal care and dedication.

# ACKNOWLEDGMENTS

There is never enough room to acknowledge every person. Many people contributed to my perspective about veterinary medicine, assisted in the development of my knowledge base, or taught me indelible lessons. In a lifetime of experiences working with students, I am wiser and more worldly.

I gratefully acknowledge Michelle Tahan, Jasmine Jhunjhnuwala, and E. Liz Kim, as well as my family, friends, colleagues, and professors. It is with profound gratitude that I mention and acknowledge the many animal owners I have known.

As a faculty member in the UCLA College Counseling Certificate Program, I met many dedicated counselors who spend their life serving and supporting students. Meaningful contributions to the book have been made indirectly by admissions representatives, college counselors, faculty members who took a special interest in this book's success.

I would also like to thank the thousands of students I have taught, counseled, or supported in my nearly four decades of service.

Isaac Newton once said, "If I see so far, it is because I stand on the shoulders of giants."

A few of those giants whose broad shoulders lifted me higher and helped teach invaluable lessons include: David, Malka, and Steven Waugh, Jerry, Gail, and Robert Waugh, Leonard/Roberta Mirvis, Zenobia Miro, Harrison White, Sandy Greenspun, Shawna Bahri, Maddie Browning, Katie Foose, Jack Grieder, Michael Chian, Anila Baseel, Jennifer Pearson, Candice Katayama, Karyn Holtzman, Jik Lee, Deb Ferber, Suzanne Crawford, David LeBoff, Steve and Debby Kurti, Michael Castro, Sasha Dastmalchi, Maha Shah, Stark Zhang, David and Kathy Krebs, Fred Feldon, Briana Flores, Rochelle Wilder, and James Sullivan.

Finally, there would be no book on vet school and no career college admissions counseling, without the support of Robert Helmer whose tireless efforts support me every single day.

> *"If I see so far, it is because I stand on the shoulders of giants."*
> *— Isaac Newton*

# ABOUT THE AUTHOR

D r. Rachel A. Winston is a tireless student advocate. She has served the educational community as a university professor, college advisor, statistician, researcher, author, cryptanalyst, motivational speaker, publishing executive, and lifelong student. As one of the leading experts in college counseling and an award-winning faculty member, Dr. Winston has spent her lifetime learning, teaching, mentoring, and coaching students. Much of her counseling practice is focused on admissions to medical, dental, vet, and engineering schools.

She started college at thirteen and graduated from college programs in such widely ranging disciplines as chemistry, mathematics, computers, liberal arts, international relations, negotiation, conflict resolution, peacebuilding, business administration, higher education leadership, interpreting, college counseling, and publishing. Throughout her education, she attended Harvard, UChicago, NYU, GWU, Syracuse, Maryland, UCLA, UCI, CSUF, CSUDH, Cal Poly, ASU, Claremont Graduate University, Pepperdine, and USC among other colleges.

Her position working in Washington, D.C. on Capitol Hill and with the White House in the 1980s took her to approximately a hundred universities training campaign managers at colleges from Colorado to California, thoroughly dotting the western states. Later, she led college tours with students and their families on road trips throughout the United States. She has taught or counseled thousands of students over her career and speaks at conferences and academic programs throughout the world.

As a professor and avid writer for numerous publications, she won the 2012 McFarland Literary Achievement Award, Bletchley Park Cryptanalyst Award, and numerous other awards, including Faculty Member of the Year, Leadership Tomorrow Leader of the Year, and college service and leadership awards. While studying Human Capital at Claremont Graduate University, she was a scholarship recipient at the Drucker School of Management. She was also elected to the statewide Board of Governors for the Faculty Association for California Community Colleges, where she served on their executive committee.

She served as a faculty member for the UCLA College Counselor Certificate Program, the Director of Mathematics at Brandman University, and Embry Riddle Aeronautical University, Chapman University, Cal State Fullerton, and a handful of California Community Colleges, including Cerro Coso College where she also served as the Academic Senate President and retired in 2016. Over her career, she taught mathematics online, on television, live interactive satellite, telecourses, and in large and small lecture halls.

# AUTHOR'S NOTE

You are reading this book because you are considering admission to vet school. Whatever route you took to get to this point, you are in the right place. Right now, you need to gather information to make informed decisions.

While many people offer advice, suggestions differ. Friends will tell you the 'right' way or the way their neighbor was accepted. Graciously accept this anecdotal information while you commit to learning more. This opportunity to pursue veterinary medicine is your future.

Dig deeper to consider both expert and current information from counselors who have worked with hundreds of students. Changes in programs, curricula, requirements, and links happen each year.

Doublecheck each program's specifics yourself. This guide is current as of September 2021, with each school's profile information. However, since researching this book, changes may have taken place. There are other vet school books written by talented and experienced counselors. We admire and cheer on their efforts.

> *"We are what we think. All that we are arises with our thoughts. With our thoughts, we make the world."*
> — *Buddha*

This set of profiles and lists is different in that it also provides and unique tidbits. We hope you find this information valuable. Your job is to begin early by assembling information for the schools you are considering. Create a road map and set yourself on a clear path.

If you see an error in this book or even a suggestion for a future edition, please write to Rachel Winston at collegeguide@yahoo.com. We will fix the entry with the next printed version. All of that said, this book was written for you in mind.

There is a wealth of information on the Internet with free downloads, FAQs, testimonials, and offers to help you with your applications. Some of these advisors are knowledgeable and could help you. Students and parents hunt around the web, searching for a tremendous number of hours to seek the information they need.

This book of profiles was designed to make your search easier. For now, though, we will assume that you are reasonably confident that you want to attend vet school and are exploring this avenue as a possible way to take advantage of a program that will get you on your way toward your goal.

We assume that you are a highly academic candidate who is willing to work very hard. You may be fascinated with the human body, animal physiology, or healing. Serving others selflessly is virtually a prerequisite for veterinary medical programs.

As you investigate colleges, you might find that some schools call these VMD or DVM programs; either way, this book will help you get to your goal. Applying to and writing essays for each application will require research to determine which is right for you.

While you might believe that vet programs are relatively similar, each program's nuances make them very different. These small differences may seem confusing. Our goal with this book is to demystify the information and process.

# CONTENTS

CHAPTER 1

# VETERINARY COLLEGES OF MEDICINE AND THE PANDEMIC

*"Personally, I have always felt that the best doctor is the veterinarian. He can't ask his patients what is the matter... he's just got to know."*
*– Will Rogers*

## RESILIENCE AND FLEXIBILITY

During the COVID-19 pandemic, life as we knew it changed. The public health crisis impacted colleges worldwide, including the way classes were taught, training for veterinary medical students, and undergraduate and graduate admissions. Admissions offices granted some flexibility to applicants throughout the process as local, state, and national requirements for masking, vaccines, distancing, and classroom access shifted with the winds.

As schools adapted, students and applicants adapted as well. Students attempted to take the GRE multiple times as test centers opened and closed. Research facilities did not allow lab assistants to work in the building, resulting in discussion-based journal clubs to suffice for laboratory experiences. Some attempted to gain work and volunteer experiences with limited success. Even getting letters of recommendation became difficult as professors refused to write letters for students they had never met in person.

Resilience cannot be understated. Vet school applicants could not base their future on their past as the ground shifted underneath. With schools going test-optional, schools offering classes online, and, volunteer opportunities shutting down, virtually all of the traditional requirements changed. Work experience is nearly a prerequisite to some vet schools. However, animal care facilities had to adjust to patient needs and government regulations which often barred pet owners from entering and volunteers from assisting. Suddenly there was a 'new normal' with ever-changing rules.

Similarly, faculty needed to continue 'as usual' in transformed classroom environments that alternated from online to in-person classes as students, faculty, and staff adapted to COVID-19 requirements. Weekly and sometimes daily rapid COVID tests were administered. Meanwhile, classrooms filled with masked faces of socially distanced students managing their own challenges while complying to those of schools

Admissions officers who presented at college fairs now discussed their schools virtually. Those representatives who traveled to colleges to meet with prospective students or gave tours on campus needed to find alternatives. Most interviews were conducted virtually, some with multiple interviewees in group interview days. Every participant in the vet school admissions ecosystem needed to find new ways to both reach out to student applicants and interview candidates.

One of the most interesting aspects taking hold at some schools is artificial intelligence initial screening of applicants. In addition, a few vet schools do not meet their candidates at all and choose students without an interview. While these changes may or may not stick, they are with us now at some schools and are likely to take root in the new normal of vet school admissions.

**Pass/Fail Grades** – Most veterinary medical schools are accepting P/F grades for specific terms only. Check with each school.

**Online Prerequisite Courses** – Courses that transitioned to online during specific terms only will be counted. Otherwise, online courses may not be accepted for credit.

**Standardized Tests** – Some schools are test-optional, and some still require the test. The test does not need to be submitted with the initial application, thereby allowing students to find a convenient time to take the test. However, most require the test to be submitted by September 15 for the upcoming year's admissions.

**CASPer Testing** – As of August 2021, veterinary medical schools requiring CASPer for 2022 admissions include (check schools for any changes):

| | |
|---|---|
| Kansas State University | Ross University (St. Kitts) |
| Lincoln Memorial University | Texas Tech |
| Long Island University | UC Davis |
| Michigan State University | University of Florida |
| Oklahoma State University | Virginia-Maryland College of Veterinary Medicine |
| Purdue University | |

**GRE Testing** – As of August 2021, veterinary medical schools requiring the GRE for 2022 admissions include (check schools for any changes):

| | |
|---|---|
| Auburn University | Ross University (St. Kitts) |
| Louisiana State University | Tuskeegee University |
| Oklahoma State University | UC Davis |

For the most part, the timeline stayed the same. My advice is to start just after the New Year to familiarize yourself with the Veterinary Medical School Admissions Requirements (VMSAR). Much of the information is somewhat difficult to download and either print or save. However, there is a significant amount of data available. Go to *https://applytovetschool.org*.

Also, give someone your essays to read over ahead of time. You want to submit so you are ahead or on time rather than applying late.

There are two admissions systems for veterinary medical school that are not interconnected. The Veterinary Medical College Application Service (VMCAS) contains the applications for 31 of the 33 vet schools. The remaining two school applications for the two schools located in Texas are found at Texas Medical and Dental Schools Application Service (TMDSAS).

## VET ADMISSIONS TIMELINE

### January 2021

- Become familiar with the application process and veterinary schools. Good sources of information are the Veterinary Medical School Admissions Requirements (VMSAR) database: https://applytovetschool.org/, school websites, and your pre-health advisor.
- VMCAS is available online January 21. Although you can begin filling out the application immediately, you cannot select and submit applications to programs until May 12. The VMCAS is not due until September 15.
- Continue to gain veterinary, animal, community service and/or research experience throughout this year and next year.

### February – March 2021

- Letters of Recommendation – Who will write your letters? For letters of recommendation from your professors, request these before school ends for the year. Sooner is better than later since some faculty do not work during the summer. Also, the number and type of recommendations vary by school. For example, many vet schools require three letters, with at least one letter from a veterinarian and one from a professor (sometimes specifically a science professor).
- Focus on classes, research, and veterinary experiences.

### April – May 2021

- Prepare for and take the GRE if you plan to take it in the spring.
- TMDSAS opens on May 1.
- May 12 – Vet school programs are available for selection on VMCAS. Fill out program-specific supplemental questions. The application can be submitted at this time. Still, most veterinary schools do not have rolling admissions, so it can be beneficial to wait until after completing summer veterinary, animal, and research experiences and/or summer school to include those on the application.

**June – August 2021**

- Summer veterinary, animal, research, or other experiences.
- Take additional classes in subjects that are recommended by colleges.
- Prepare for and take GRE if not already completed.
- Develop your VMCAS supplemental application essays.

**September 2021**

- September 15 is VMCAS and TMDSAS deadline.

**October 2021 – February 2022**

- Interviews begin as early as October at some schools and then continue until February, although some schools may interview into early spring.

**Fall 2022**

- Begin vet school! You are on your way!

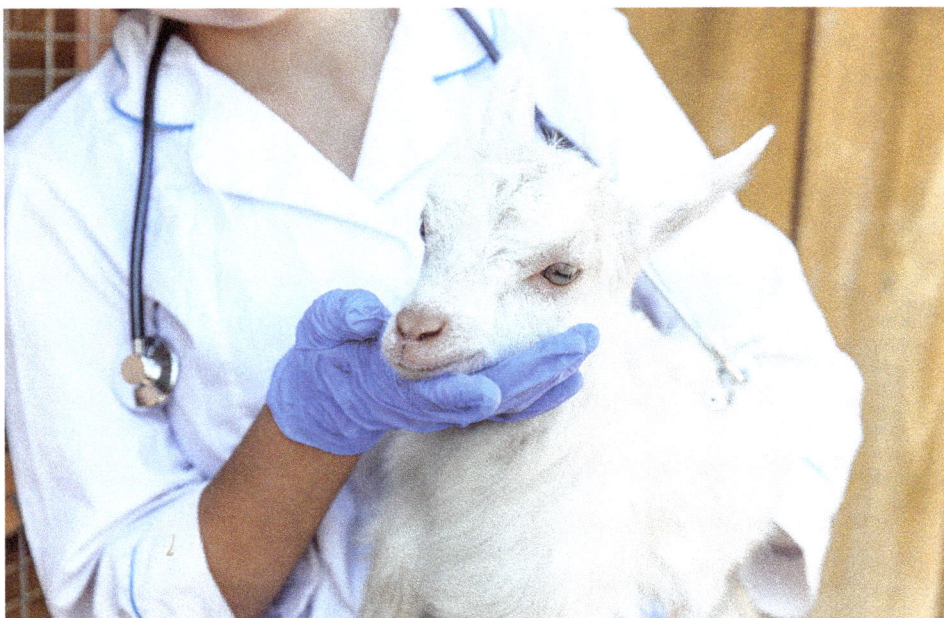

# PROFILES AND LISTS

The profiles and tables in this book include information available in the summer of 2021 for the fall of 2022. Outside of fee increases and new programs, changes in admission are unlikely to be significant through 2024 since many students who apply in 2024 were in college in 2020 and 2021, during which the pandemic impacted coursework.

Notably, the demand for veterinarians and the desire for students to pursue vet school has increased. There was a significant change in the number of applicants for fall 2021, which is likely to result in lower acceptance rates and an increase in GPAs and test score averages. A record 20% more students applied to veterinary medical school for 2021. Given the importance of valuable information about schools, lists, and profiles, this book will prove extremely helpful to those wanting to make solid decisions.

With data about applicants, admitted students, and entering classes, along with tests, requirements, and contacts, you have the information here at your fingertips. The companion book to this profile book offers more specific information about vet school planning, GPA, eLOR, resumes, vet experiences, research, prerequisites, timelines, applications, essays, international programs, financial aid, scholarships. Vet school is the right place if you have a keen interest in animal anatomy and physiology, disease diagnostics, zoology, entomology, food security, and/or pet/livestock/aquatic animal welfare.

The profiles are laid out by region with location markers in the general location of the school. Some of the vet schools are in more rural regions, while others are in cities. No doubt, the demand is high in both areas. In many areas, there are grave shortages of veterinarians. Whether you work for an animal hospital, an association, USDA, FDA, NIH, CDC, the U.S. Army Corps, or open your own clinic, you will find a career waiting for you when you graduate.

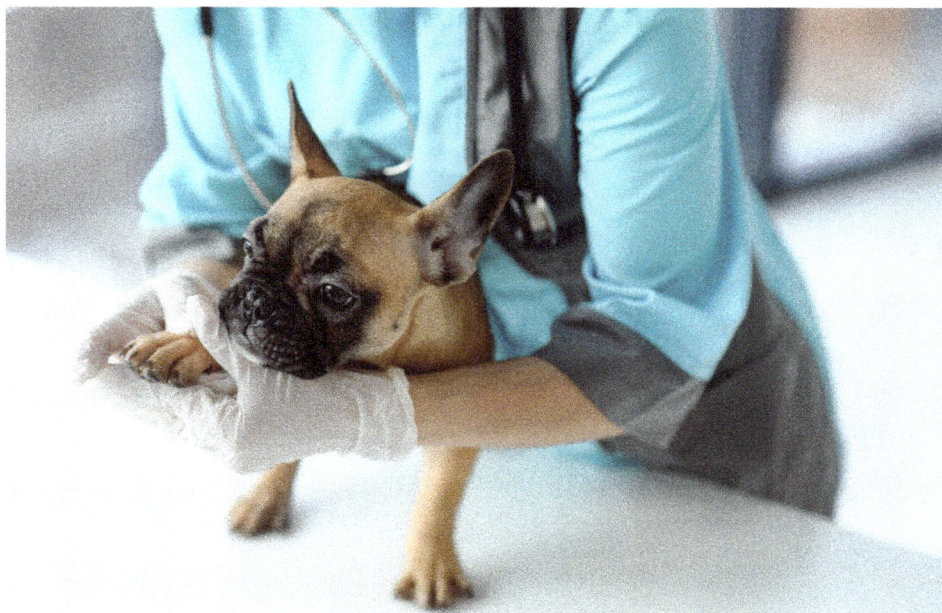

**4**
Regions

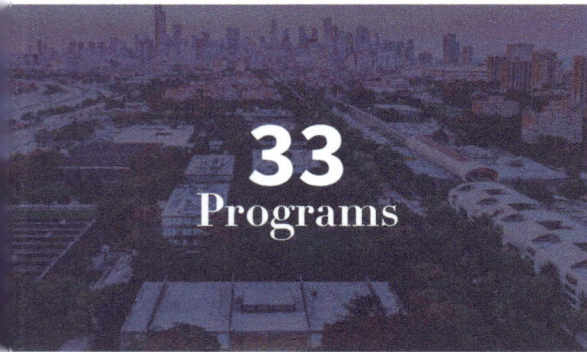

**33**
Programs

# COLLEGE PROFILES AND REQUIREMENTS

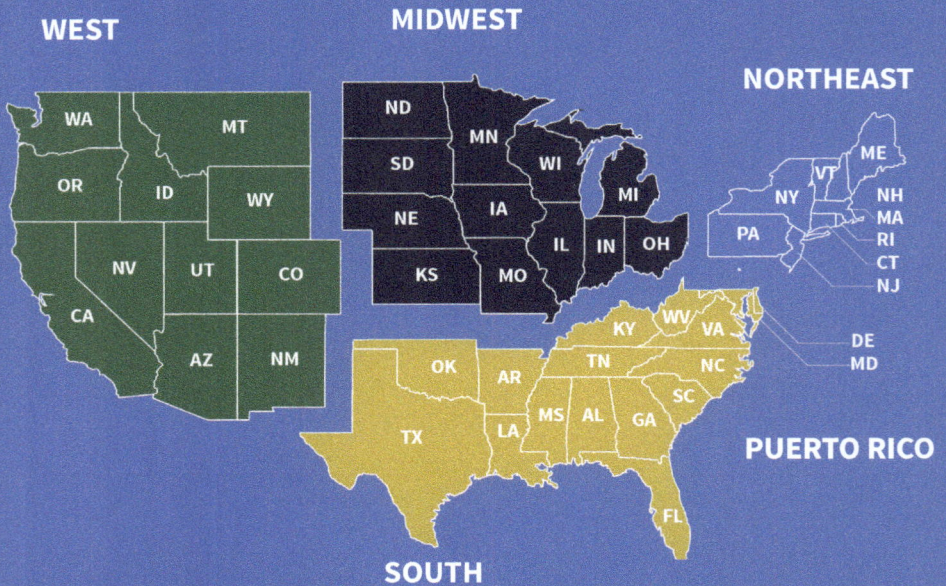

WEST

MIDWEST

NORTHEAST

SOUTH

PUERTO RICO

# VET PROGRAMS BY REGION
## U.S. CENSUS BUREAU CLASSIFICATIONS

### REGION 1 – NORTHEAST

Connecticut, Maine, Massachusetts, New Hampshire, New Jersey, New York, Pennsylvania, Rhode Island, and Vermont

### REGION 2 – MIDWEST

Illinois, Indiana, Iowa, Kansas, Michigan, Minnesota, Missouri, Nebraska, North Dakota, Ohio, South Dakota, and Wisconsin

### REGION 3 – SOUTH

Alabama, Arkansas, Delaware, District of Columbia, Florida, Georgia, Kentucky, Louisiana, Maryland, Mississippi, North Carolina, Oklahoma, South Carolina, Tennessee, Texas, Virginia, and West Virginia

### REGION 4 – WEST

Alaska, Arizona, California, Colorado, Hawaii, Idaho, Montana, Nevada, New Mexico, Oregon, Utah, Washington, and Wyoming

# LIST OF VET PROGRAMS

T he programs listed in the following pages contain veterinary school programs. Following this list, this book provides lists of MD, DO, dental, PharmD, and DMD/DDS schools, since many students interested in medical school are also interested in healthcare. There are many facets of the healthcare world. One of these other areas might be a good option for you.

Vet school is not for everyone.

Thus, this book aims to provide you with a more comprehensive set of lists so that you can explore your options. Keep the book handy. You may find that even after you begin college, if you choose a traditional pre-vet path, you may find the list of additional programs in the back a good option for you.

Lists are often tedious to find and take a while to pull together. These lists were gathered to help you with this task.

Descriptions of the college programs, tuition, requirements, and deadlines are accurate as of April 2021. Requirements may have changed somewhat due to the pandemic, but all of this information is a great place to start!

Note: To simplify the text and fit information into the charts and descriptions, abbreviations were used as well as shortened sentences and acronyms.

CHAPTER 2

## REGION ONE

# NORTHEAST

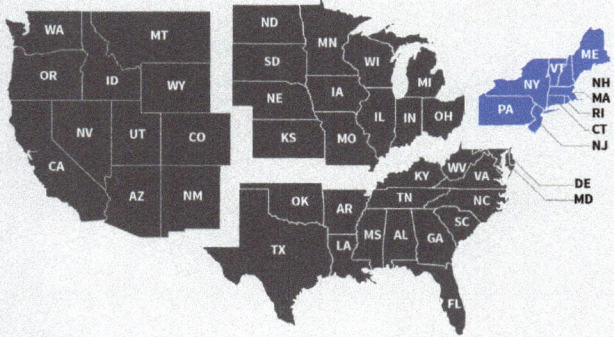

**CONNECTICUT**

**MAINE**

**MASSACHUSETTS**

**NEW HAMPSHIRE**

**NEW JERSEY**

**NEW YORK**

**PENNSYLVANIA**

**RHODE ISLAND**

**VERMONT**

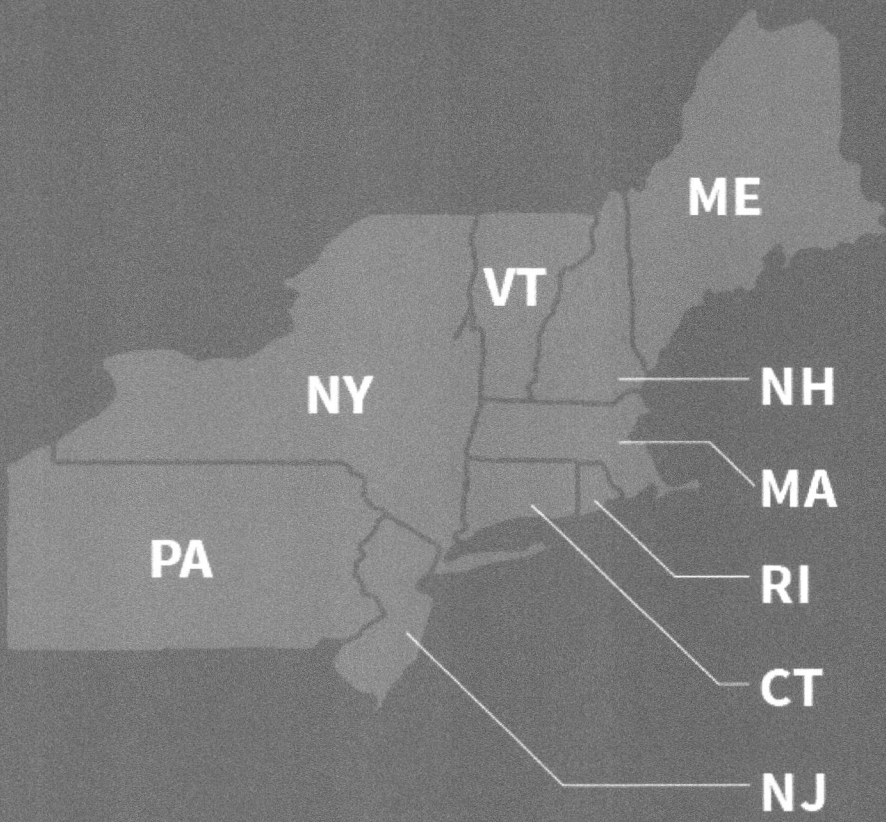

# 4 Programs | 9 States

1. *MA – Tufts University School of Veterinary Medicine*
2. *NY - Cornell University College of Veterinary Medicine*
3. *NY - Long Island University School of Veterinary Medicine*
4. *PA - University of Pennsylvania School of Veterinary Medicine*

# VETERINARY PROGRAMS

| Veterinary School | Ave. GPA & GRE / Early Decision (Ed) : Yes/No / Int'l Students: Yes/No / Reapps: Yes/No | Admissions Statistics | Science Req. Other than Gen Chem, OChem, Physics, Bio |
|---|---|---|---|
| **Tufts University**<br><br>200 Westboro Rd, North Grafton, MA 01536 | 3.72 (overall)<br>3.51 (science)<br><br>GRE:<br>158 (V)<br>157 (Q)<br><br>ED: No<br><br>Int'l Student: Yes<br><br>Reapps: Yes | **(2019)**<br>Apps Received: 936<br>Interview Received: 400<br>Number Enrolled: 100<br>Admitted Rate: 10.7%<br><br>**(2020)**<br>Apps Received: 826<br>Interview Received: 400<br>Number Enrolled: 105<br>Admitted Rate: 12.7% | Genetics<br>Biochemistry<br>Math<br>Social/Behavioral Sci. |
| **Cornell University**<br><br>602 Tower Rd, Ithaca, NY 14853 | 3.73 (overall)<br><br>GRE:<br>Not Required<br><br>ED: No<br><br>Int'l Student: Yes<br><br>Reapps: Yes | **(2019)**<br>Apps Received: N/A<br>Interview Received: N/A<br>Number Enrolled: 120<br>Admitted Rate: N/A<br><br>**(2020)**<br>Apps Received: N/A<br>Interview Received: N/A<br>Number Enrolled: 120<br>Admitted Rate: N/A | Biochemistry<br>Advanced Life Sciences |
| **Long Island University**<br><br>720 Northern Blvd., Brookville, NY 11548 | 3.4 (overall)<br><br>GRE:<br>Not Required<br><br>ED: No<br><br>Int'l Student: Yes<br><br>Reapps: N/A | **(2019)**<br>N/A<br><br>**(2020)**<br>Apps Received: 1,117<br>Interview Received: 400<br>Number Enrolled: 100<br>Admitted Rate: 9.0% | Biochemistry<br>Math or Statistics<br>Genetics<br>English Composition<br>Public Speaking |

| Veterinary School | Ave. GPA & GRE<br><br>Early Decision (Ed) : Yes/No<br><br>Int'l Students: Yes/No<br><br>Reapps: Yes/No | Admissions Statistics | Science Req. Other than Gen Chem, OChem, Physics, Bio |
|---|---|---|---|
| **University of Pennsylvania**<br><br>3800 Spruce St, Philadelphia, PA 19104 | 3.6 (overall)<br><br>GRE:<br>157 (V)<br>157 (Q)<br><br>ED: No<br><br>Int'l Student: Yes<br><br>Reapps: N/A | **(2019)**<br>Apps Received: 1,300<br>Interview Received: N/A<br>Number Enrolled: 122<br>Admitted Rate: 9.38%<br><br>**(2020)**<br>Apps Received: 1,146<br>Interview Received: 280<br>Number Enrolled: 127<br>Admitted Rate: 11.08% | Microbiology<br>Biochemistry<br>Calculus<br>Statistics |

**NORTHEAST**

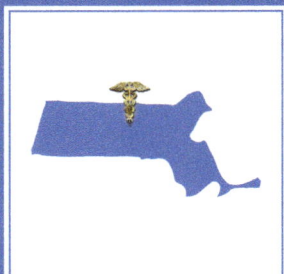

CONNECTICUT

MAINE

**MASSACHUSETTS**

NEW HAMPSHIRE

NEW JERSEY

NEW YORK

PENNSYLVANIA

RHODE ISLAND

VERMONT

# TUFTS UNIVERSITY SCHOOL OF VETERINARY MEDICINE

**Address:** 200 Westboro Rd, North Grafton, MA 01536
**Website:** *https://vet.tufts.edu/*
**Contact:** *https://vet.admissions.tufts.edu/register/requestforinfo*
**Phone:** (508) 839-7920

## COST OF ATTENDANCE

**Tuition:** $60,694
**Fees & Expenses:** $24,582
**Total:** $82,276
**Financial Aid:** https://vet.tufts.edu/admissions/financial-aid/

## ADDITIONAL INFORMATION

**Interesting tidbit:** Cummings Veterinary Medical Center at Tufts comprises seven hospitals and clinics. From their first year onward, students gain valuable expertise and enjoy a rich clinical learning environment.

**Important Updates due to COVID-19:** Due to the coronavirus pandemic, applicants do not need approval from the admissions office to take online coursework to fulfill prerequisite courses for the 2020-21 academic year.

**Were tests required?** No.

**Are tests expected next year?** No.

**What percent of admitted students participate in international experiences?** N/A, International Veterinary Medicine certificate program available.

**What percent of current students take an extra year for research or a dual degree?** 7% dual degree. For more information on dual degree options, visit: https://vet.tufts.edu/education/combined-dvm-programs/

**What service learning opportunities exist?** https://vet.tufts.edu/community/volunteer-opportunities-cummings/

**NAVLE First-Time Pass Rate:** 100% (2019)

# CORNELL UNIVERSITY COLLEGE OF VETERINARY MEDICINE

**Address:** 602 Tower Rd, Ithaca, NY 14853
**Website:** *https://www.vet.cornell.edu/*
**Contact:** *https://www.vet.cornell.edu/about-us/contact-us*
**Phone:** (607) 253-3000

## COST OF ATTENDANCE

**In-State Tuition:** $39,206
**Fees & Expenses:** $19,500
**Total:** $58,706

**Out-of-State Tuition:** $58,244
**Fees & Expenses:** $19,500
**Total:** $77,744

**Financial Aid:** https://www.vet.cornell.edu/education/doctor-veterinary-medicine/financing-your-veterinary-education/scholarships

## ADDITIONAL INFORMATION

**Interesting tidbit:** CU College of Veterinary Medicine is a state-supported college at Cornell University. It has 7 teaching hospitals, 5 academic departments, 4 research centers and 43 clinical specialties.

**Important Updates due to COVID-19:** Contact DVM Admissions Office for questions. GRE'S (and MCAT's) are no longer required to apply to Cornell starting with the 2020 application cycle and all future application cycles going forward.

**Were tests required?** No.

**Are tests expected next year?** No.

**What percent of admitted students participate in international experiences?** N/A

**What percent of current students take an extra year for research or a dual degree?** 11.6% dual degree. For more information on these programs, visit: https://www.vet.cornell.edu/education/doctor-veterinary-medicine/admissions/combined-degree-programs

**What service learning opportunities exist?** https://www.vet.cornell.edu/about-us/outreach

**NAVLE First-Time Pass Rate:** 97% (2020)

CONNECTICUT

MAINE

MASSACHUSETTS

NEW HAMPSHIRE

NEW JERSEY

NEW YORK

PENNSYLVANIA

RHODE ISLAND

VERMONT

**NORTHEAST**

# LONG ISLAND UNIVERSITY COLLEGE OF VETERINARY MEDICINE

**Address:** 720 Northern Boulevard, Brookville, NY 11548
**Website:** *https://liu.edu/vetmed*
**Contact:** *https://liu.edu/vetmed/about/contact-us*
**Phone:** (516) 299-3679

## COST OF ATTENDANCE

**Tuition:** $56,100
**Fees & Expenses:** $31,497
**Total:** $87,597

**Financial Aid:** https://liu.edu/VetMed/Education/Doctor-of-Veterinary-Medicine/Financial-Aid

## ADDITIONAL INFORMATION

**Interesting tidbit:** LIU-CVM offers a combination of a traditional curriculum, with unique courses such as Veterinary Skills and Integrations, that weave clinical cases into all stages of the curriculum. The College is built on a solid foundation of biomedical research. The inaugural class began the DVM program in Fall 2020.

**Important Updates due to COVID-19:** Online coursework from all accredited programs will be accepted. Courses with pass/fail grading will be accepted as long as the student receives a pass. The public speaking requirement is waived for the 2020-2021 and 2021-2022 admission cycles.

**Were tests required?** No.

**Are tests expected next year?** No.

**What percent of admitted students participate in international experiences?** N/A

**What percent of current students take an extra year for research or a dual degree?** N/A

**What service learning opportunities exist?** N/A

**NAVLE First-Time Pass Rate:** N/A (inaugural class matriculated in Fall 2020)

CONNECTICUT

MAINE

MASSACHUSETTS

NEW HAMPSHIRE

NEW JERSEY

NEW YORK

PENNSYLVANIA

RHODE ISLAND

VERMONT

# UNIVERSITY OF PENNSYLVANIA SCHOOL OF VETERINARY MEDICINE

**Address:** 3800 Spruce St, Philadelphia, PA 19104
**Website:** *https://www.vet.upenn.edu/*
**Contact:** *https://www.vet.upenn.edu/people/contact-penn-vet/contact*
**Phone:** (215) 898-5434

## COST OF ATTENDANCE

**In-State Tuition:** $59,278
**Fees & Expenses:** $25,034
**Total:** $84,312

**Out-of-State Tuition:** $69,278
**Fees & Expenses:** $25,034
**Total:** $94,312

**Financial Aid:** https://www.vet.upenn.edu/education/vmd-admissions/paying-for-your-education/financial-assistance

## ADDITIONAL INFORMATION

**Interesting tidbit:** Penn Vet is the only veterinary school developed in association with a medical school, and is one of only four private veterinary schools in the nation.

**Important Updates due to COVID-19:** Penn Vet has always accepted online coursework from accredited colleges/universities. If a college/university is only allowing students to take courses Pass/Fail, we will accept a Pass in any Spring, Summer, Fall 2020, or Spring and Summer 2021 course to meet a requirement(s).

**Were tests required?** Penn Vet will no longer require (or accept) the GRE as part of the application process.

**Are tests expected next year?** No.

**What percent of admitted students participate in international experiences?** N/A

**What percent of current students take an extra year for research or a dual degree?** 20.5% dual degree. For more information on these programs, visit: https://www.vet.upenn.edu/education/dual-degree-programs

**What service learning opportunities exist?** Shelter Medicine: https://www.vet.upenn.edu/research/centers-initiatives/shelter-medicine/partners-in-outreach

**NAVLE First-Time Pass Rate:** 97% (2020)

CONNECTICUT

MAINE

MASSACHUSETTS

NEW HAMPSHIRE

NEW JERSEY

NEW YORK

PENNSYLVANIA

RHODE ISLAND

VERMONT

**NORTHEAST**

ILLINOIS

INDIANA

IOWA

KANSAS

MICHIGAN

MINNESOTA

MISSOURI

NEBRASKA

NORTH DAKOTA

OHIO

SOUTH DAKOTA

WISCONSIN

## CHAPTER 3
# REGION TWO
# MIDWEST

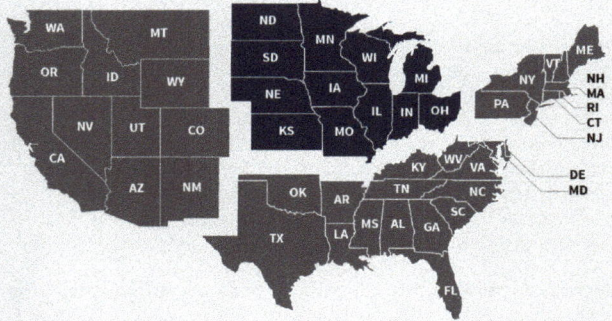

# 9 *Programs* | 12 *States*

1. IL – University of Illinois College of Veterinary Medicine
2. IN – Purdue University College of Veterinary Medicine
3. IA – Iowa State University College of Veterinary Medicine
4. KS – Kansas State University College of Veterinary Medicine
5. MI – Michigan State University College of Veterinary Medicine
6. MN – University of Minnesota College of Veterinary Medicine
7. MO – University of Missouri - Columbia College of Veterinary Medicine
8. OH – The Ohio State University College of Veterinary Medicine
9. WI – University of Wisconsin-Madison School of Veterinary Medicine

# VETERINARY PROGRAMS

| Veterinary School | Avg. GPA & GRE<br><br>Early Decision (ED): Yes/No<br><br>Int'l Students: Yes/No<br><br>Reapps: Yes/No | Admissions Statistics | Science Req. Other than Gen Chem, OChem, Physics, Bio |
|---|---|---|---|
| **University of Illinois**<br><br>2001 S Lincoln Ave, Urbana, IL 61802 | 3.59 (overall)<br>3.49 (science)<br><br>GRE: 63%<br><br>ED: No<br><br>Int'l Student: Yes<br><br>Reapps: N/A | **(2019)**<br>Apps Received: 900<br>Interview Received: 350<br>Number Enrolled: 130<br>Admitted Rate: 14.4%<br><br>**(2020)**<br>Apps Received: 1,003<br>Interview Received: 373<br>Number Enrolled: 130<br>Admitted Rate: 13.0% | Humanities/Social Science Science Electives |
| **Purdue University**<br><br>625 Harrison St, West Lafayette, IN 47907 | 3.74 (resident)<br>3.67 (non-resident)<br><br>GRE: Not Required<br><br>ED: No<br><br>Int'l Student: Yes<br><br>Reapps: Yes | **(2019)**<br>Apps Received: 1,468<br>Interview Received: 300<br>Number Enrolled: 87<br>Admitted Rate: 5.92%<br><br>**(2020)**<br>Apps Received: 1,649<br>Interview Received: 300<br>Number Enrolled: 84<br>Admitted Rate: 5.09% | N/A |
| **Iowa State University**<br><br>1800 Christensen Dr., Ames, IA 50011 | 3.54 (overall)<br><br>GRE: Not Required<br><br>ED: No<br><br>Int'l Student: Yes<br><br>Reapps: Yes | **(2019)**<br>Apps Received: N/A<br>Interview Received: Discontinued<br>Number Enrolled: 154<br>Admitted Rate: N/A<br><br>**(2020)**<br>Apps Received: 1,685<br>Interview Received: Not Required<br>Number Enrolled: 157<br>Admitted Rate: 9.32% | Genetics/Animal Breeding Anatomy/Physiology Arts/Humanities/Social Sci. Electives |

# VETERINARY PROGRAMS

| Veterinary School | Avg. GPA & GRE<br><br>Early Decision (ED): Yes/No<br><br>Int'l Students: Yes/No<br><br>Reapps: Yes/No | Admissions Statistics | Science Req. Other than Gen Chem, OChem, Physics, Bio |
|---|---|---|---|
| **Kansas State University**<br><br>1710 Denison Ave, Manhattan, KS 66502 | 3.67 (overall)<br>3.51 (science)<br><br>GRE:<br>Not Required<br><br>ED: No<br><br>Int'l Student: Yes<br><br>Reapps: Yes | **(2019)**<br>Apps Received: N/A<br>Interview Received: N/A<br>Number Enrolled: 112<br>Admitted Rate: N/A<br><br>**(2020)**<br>Apps Received: 971<br>Interview Received: 495<br>Number Enrolled: 124<br>Admitted Rate: 12.8% | Microbiology<br>Genetics<br>Social Sciences<br>Electives |
| **Michigan State University**<br><br>784 Wilson Rd Room G-100, East Lansing, MI 48824 | 3.32 (science)<br><br>GRE:<br>Not Required<br><br>ED: No<br><br>Int'l Student: Yes<br><br>Reapps: Yes | **(2019)**<br>Apps Received: 1,963<br>Interview Received: 288<br>Number Enrolled: 115<br>Admitted Rate: 5.86%<br><br>**(2020)**<br>Apps Received: 1,963<br>Interview Received: 288<br>Number Enrolled: 116<br>Admitted Rate: 5.91% | College Alg. & Trig. or Pre-calc or Calc.<br>Biochemistry<br>Upper Level Biology<br>Social Sciences |
| **University of Minnesota**<br><br>1365 Gortner Ave, St Paul, MN 55108 | 3.76 (science)<br><br>GRE:<br>155 (V)<br>160 (Q)<br><br>ED: No<br><br>Int'l Student: Yes<br><br>Reapps: Yes | **(2019)**<br>Apps Received: 950<br>Interview Received: N/A<br>Number Enrolled: 105<br>Admitted Rate: 11%<br><br>**(2020)**<br>Apps Received: 959<br>Interview Received: N/A<br>Number Enrolled: 105<br>Admitted Rate: 10.95% | Zoology w/ Lab<br>Microbiology w/ Lab<br>Genetics<br>Biochemistry |

**MIDWEST**

# VETERINARY PROGRAMS

| Veterinary School | Avg. GPA & GRE<br><br>Early Decision (ED): Yes/No<br><br>Int'l Students: Yes/No<br><br>Reapps: Yes/No | Admissions Statistics | Science Req. Other than Gen Chem, OChem, Physics, Bio |
|---|---|---|---|
| **University of Missouri**<br><br>900 E Campus Dr, Columbia, MO 65211 | 3.74 (overall)<br><br>GRE:<br>Not Required<br><br>ED: No<br><br>Int'l Student: Yes<br><br>Reapps: Yes | **(2019)**<br>Apps Received: 1,240<br>Interview Received: N/A<br>Number Enrolled: 120<br>Admitted Rate: 9.7%<br><br>**(2020)**<br>Apps Received: 1,222<br>Interview Received: 348<br>Number Enrolled: 124<br>Admitted Rate: 10.2% | Biochemistry<br>Genetics, Microbio., Anatomy, or Physio. |
| **Ohio State University**<br><br>1900 Coffey Rd, Columbus, OH 43210 | 3.6 (overall)<br><br>GRE:<br>Not Required<br><br>ED: No<br><br>Int'l Student: Yes<br><br>Reapps: N/A | **(2019)**<br>Apps Received: 1,389<br>Interview Received: 507<br>Number Enrolled: 162<br>Admitted Rate: 11.7%<br><br>**(2020)**<br>Apps Received: 2,415<br>Interview Received: 575<br>Number Enrolled: 162<br>Admitted Rate: 6.71% | Biochemistry<br>Microbio. w/ Lab<br>Physiology<br>Science Electives<br>Humanities/Social Sci. |
| **Univ. of Wisconsin-Madison**<br><br>2015 Linden Dr., Madison, WI 53706 | **Resident:**<br>3.68 (overall)<br>3.70 (science)<br><br>**Non-resident:**<br>3.66 (overall)<br>3.67 (science)<br><br>GRE:<br>Not Required<br><br>ED: No<br><br>Int'l Student: Yes<br><br>Reapps: N/A | **(2019)**<br>Apps Received: 1,218<br>Interview Received: N/A<br>Number Enrolled: 96<br>Admitted Rate: 7.3%<br><br>**(2020)**<br>Apps Received: 1,267<br>Interview Received: N/A<br>Number Enrolled: 96<br>Admitted Rate: 7.58% | Biology or Zoology<br>Genetics or Animal Breed.<br>Qualitative Chem.<br>Biochemistry<br>Statistics<br>Social Sci./Humanities |

# UNIVERSITY OF ILLINOIS COLLEGE OF VETERINARY MEDICINE

**Address:** 2001 S Lincoln Ave, Urbana, IL 61802
**Website:** *https://vetmed.illinois.edu/*
**Contact:** *https://vetmed.illinois.edu/about/contact-location/*
**Phone:** (217) 333-2760

## COST OF ATTENDANCE

**In-State Tuition:** $28,694
**Fees & Expenses:** $22,626
**Total:** $51,320

**Out-of-State Tuition:** $51,398
**Fees & Expenses:** $22,966
**Total:** $74,364

**Financial Aid:** No institutional aid for DVM students. Students should seek federal financial assistance or external scholarships through https://osfa.illinois.edu/

## ADDITIONAL INFORMATION

**Interesting tidbit:** In 2009, the faculty had conceived and implemented an innovative veterinary curriculum that integrated clinical competency throughout the four-year degree program. The innovative integrated curriculum was commended by the veterinary accreditation site visit team in 2013.

**Important Updates due to COVID-19:** Accept P/F online instruction if completed in Spring 2020 with a Passing grade.

**Were tests required?** No (GRE optional).

**Are tests expected next year?** No.

**What percent of admitted students participate in international experiences?** N/A, IVM available: https://vetmed.illinois.edu/education/doctor-veterinary-medicine-degree/illinois-veterinary-curriculum/international-programs/

**What percent of current students take an extra year for research or a dual degree?** 18.5% dual degree. For DVM/PhD dual degree option, see https://vetmed.illinois.edu/education/doctor-veterinary-medicine-degree/research-opportunities-dvm-students/veterinary-medical-scholars-program/. For DVM/MPH dual degree option, see https://vetmed.illinois.edu/education/doctor-veterinary-medicine-degree/dvm-master-public-health-degree/. Research: 10-week Summer Research Training Program available. See https://vetmed.illinois.edu/education/doctor-veterinary-medicine-degree/research-opportunities-dvm-students/summer-research-training-program/

**What service learning opportunities exist?** Shelter Medicine program: https://vetmed.illinois.edu/animal-care/shelter-medicine-program-illinois/

**NAVLE First-Time Pass Rate:** 98% (2020)

# PURDUE UNIVERSITY COLLEGE OF VETERINARY MEDICINE

**Address:** 625 Harrison St, West Lafayette, IN 47907
**Website:** *https://www.purdue.edu/vet/*
**Contact:** *https://www.purdue.edu/vet/ccc/contact.php*
**Phone:** (765) 494-7607

## COST OF ATTENDANCE

**In-State Tuition:** $19,918
**Fees & Expenses:** $16,810
**Total:** $36,796

**Out-of-State Tuition:** $44,746
**Fees & Expenses:** $17,028
**Total:** $61,556

**Financial Aid:** https://www.purdue.edu/vet/dvm/financial-aid.php

## ADDITIONAL INFORMATION

**Interesting tidbit:** In February 2020, construction crews broke ground for the college's new $108 million veterinary hospital facilities, known collectively as the David and Bonnie Brunner Purdue Veterinary Medical Hospital Complex. The new facilities will allow a 20% increase in the DVM class size, which now numbers 84.

**Important Updates due to COVID-19:** Accept P/F grading and online coursework and labs to fulfill prerequisites.

**Were tests required?** CASPer required.

**Are tests expected next year?** Yes.

**What percent of admitted students participate in international experiences?** N/A, global opportunities available: https://www.purdue.edu/vet/global/international-opportunities.php

**What percent of current students take an extra year for research or a dual degree?** N/A, dual degree options available: https://www.purdue.edu/vet/dvm/dvm-combined.php

**What service learning opportunities exist?** Priority 4 Paws program available. For more information, visit: https://www.purdue.edu/vet/priority4paws/

**NAVLE First-Time Pass Rate:** 94% (2020)

**Other:** Purdue University offers a Veterinary Scholars Program for qualified high school students to gain conditional acceptance into the DVM program. For more information, please visit: https://www.purdue.edu/vet/dvm/vet-scholars.php

ILLINOIS

INDIANA

IOWA

KANSAS

MICHIGAN

MINNESOTA

MISSOURI

NEBRASKA

NORTH DAKOTA

OHIO

SOUTH DAKOTA

WISCONSIN

**MIDWEST**

ILLINOIS

INDIANA

IOWA

KANSAS

MICHIGAN

MINNESOTA

MISSOURI

NEBRASKA

NORTH DAKOTA

OHIO

SOUTH DAKOTA

WISCONSIN

# IOWA STATE UNIVERSITY COLLEGE OF VETERINARY MEDICINE

**Address:** 1800 Christensen Drive, Ames, IA 50011
**Website:** *https://vetmed.iastate.edu/*
**Contact:** *https://vetmed.iastate.edu/vdl/about/contact-us*
**Phone:** (515) 294-1242

## COST OF ATTENDANCE

**In-State Tuition:** $24,220
**Fees & Expenses:** $54,344
**Total:** $78,564

**Out-of-State Tuition:** $53,304
**Fees & Expenses:** $83,428
**Total:** $136,732

**Financial Aid:** https://vetmed.iastate.edu/future-dvm-students/financing-your-education/scholarships

## ADDITIONAL INFORMATION

**Interesting tidbit:** Iowa State University's College of Veterinary Medicine is the nation's first public veterinary school. The college is a cornerstone of one of the world's largest concentrations of animal health professionals that includes the USDA's National Animal Disease Center, the National Veterinary Services Laboratories, and the Center for Veterinary Biologics in Ames, Iowa.

**Important Updates due to COVID-19:** Accept P/F grading for all prerequisite courses taken during the Fall/Spring/Summer 2020 and Winter/Spring 2021.

**Were tests required?** No.

**Are tests expected next year?** CASPer required.

**What percent of admitted students participate in international experiences?** N/A, study abroad encouraged: https://vetmed.iastate.edu/students/current-dvm-students/international-programs-study-abroad

**What percent of current students take an extra year for research or a dual degree?** 11.7% dual degree. For more information on these programs, visit: https://vetmed.iastate.edu/research-grad-studies/graduate-studies

**What service learning opportunities exist?** N/A

**NAVLE First-Time Pass Rate:** 96% (2020)

# KANSAS STATE UNIVERSITY COLLEGE OF VETERINARY MEDICINE

**Address:** 1710 Denison Ave, Manhattan, KS 66502
**Website:** *https://www.vet.k-state.edu/*
**Contact:** *Contact info on left side of page (in link above).*
**Phone:** (785) 532-5660

## COST OF ATTENDANCE

**In-State Tuition:** $25,746
**Fees & Expenses:** $19,728
**Total:** $45,474

**Out-of-State Tuition:** $55,742
**Fees & Expenses:** $19,728
**Total:** $75,470

**Financial Aid:** DVM students may apply for scholarships. https://www.vet.k-state.edu/admissions/financial-prep/scholarships.html

## ADDITIONAL INFORMATION

**Interesting tidbit:** The Kansas State University College of Veterinary Medicine is located within the Animal Health Corridor. The Corridor is home to more than 300 animal health companies, representing the largest concentration in the world.

**Important Updates due to COVID-19:** Accept online coursework for Spring, Summer and Fall 2020 to fulfill prerequisite requirements. Accept P/F grading for Spring and Summer 2020 to fulfill prerequisite requirements. Accept online labs for Spring, Summer and Fall 2020.

**Were tests required?** CASPer required.

**Are tests expected next year?** Yes.

**What percent of admitted students participate in international experiences?** N/A, International opportunities available. The Twinning Project is a partnership between KSU and Sokoine University of Agriculture College of Veterinary Medicine in Tanzania. Another international opportunity is the Sustainable Crop-Livestock Initiative. For more information, visit: https://www.vet.k-state.edu/international/

**What percent of current students take an extra year for research or a dual degree?** 21.4% dual degree. For more information on these programs, visit: https://www.vet.k-state.edu/education/degrees/concurrent.html Research opportunities also in the form of summer Veterinary Research Scholars Program, lab externships at Cornell University, and more.

**What service learning opportunities exist?** Shelter Medicine Program: https://www.vet.k-state.edu/vhc/services/shelter-medicine/sheltermedicine.html

**NAVLE First-Time Pass Rate:** 97% (2020)

**Other:** Early admission program available for high school students with ACT score of 29+.

ILLINOIS

INDIANA

IOWA

**KANSAS**

MICHIGAN

MINNESOTA

MISSOURI

NEBRASKA

NORTH DAKOTA

OHIO

SOUTH DAKOTA

WISCONSIN

# MIDWEST

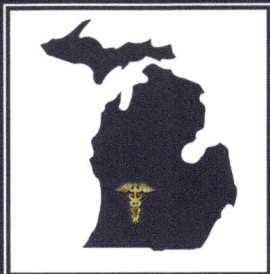

ILLINOIS

INDIANA

IOWA

KANSAS

MICHIGAN

MINNESOTA

MISSOURI

NEBRASKA

NORTH DAKOTA

OHIO

SOUTH DAKOTA

WISCONSIN

# MICHIGAN STATE UNIVERSITY COLLEGE OF VETERINARY MEDICINE

**Address:** 784 Wilson Rd Room G-100, East Lansing, MI 48824
**Website:** *https://cvm.msu.edu/*
**Contact:** *https://cvm.msu.edu/contact*
**Phone:** (517) 432-7776

## COST OF ATTENDANCE

**In-State Tuition:** $31,628
**Fees & Expenses:** $21,032
**Total:** $52,660

**Out-of-State Tuition:** $47,436
**Fees & Expenses:** $21,032
**Total:** $68,468

**Financial Aid:** https://cvm.msu.edu/students/financial-aid-and-scholarships

## ADDITIONAL INFORMATION

**Interesting tidbit:** The abundance and variety of animal agriculture and companion animals in Michigan provide the College with one of the largest clinical and diagnostic caseloads in the country. Educational and research opportunities are considerably enhanced by this large caseload.

**Important Updates due to COVID-19:** Accept grades of pass, credit, and satisfactory (binary grades) for prerequisite requirement coursework for up to seven of the 15 requirements; continue to accept online courses and labs from regionally accredited institutions.

**Were tests required?** CASPer required.

**Are tests expected next year?** Yes.

**What percent of admitted students participate in international experiences?** N/A, International Program information: https://cvm.msu.edu/about/international-programs

**What percent of current students take an extra year for research or a dual degree?** 12.3% dual degree. For more information on this program, visit: https://cvm.msu.edu/future-students/graduate-programs/dvm-phd-dual-degree-program Several summer research programs available: https://cvm.msu.edu/research/student-research/summer-research-programs

**What service learning opportunities exist?** N/A

**NAVLE First-Time Pass Rate:** 98% (2020)

**Other:** Veterinary Scholars Admissions Pathway available for MSU Honors College students seeing early admission. For more information, visit: https://cvm.msu.edu/future-students/undergraduate-programs/veterinary-scholars-admissions-pathway

# UNIVERSITY OF MINNESOTA COLLEGE OF VETERINARY MEDICINE

**Address:** 1365 Gortner Ave, St Paul, MN 55108
**Website:** https://vetmed.umn.edu/
**Contact:** https://vetmed.umn.edu/about/contact-us
**Phone:** (612) 624-6244

## COST OF ATTENDANCE

**In-State Tuition:** $32,244
**Fees & Expenses:** $18,702
**Total:** $50,946

**Out-of-State Tuition:** $57,948
 **Fees & Expenses:** $18,412
**Total:** $76,650

**Financial Aid:** https://vetmed.umn.edu/education/dvm/financial-aid

## ADDITIONAL INFORMATION

**Interesting tidbit:** The integrated DVM curriculum begins with the first three years of students focusing on the study of the normal animal, the pathogenesis of diseases, and the prevention, alleviation, and clinical therapy of diseases. The program concludes with 13 months of clinical rotations in the Veterinary Medical Center, which include more than 65 rotations ranging from Acupuncture to Zoological Medicine.

**Important Updates due to COVID-19:** Accepts online coursework to fulfill prerequisite requirements for Spring, Summer, and Fall 2020. Accepts pass/fail coursework to fulfill prerequisite requirements for spring 2020 and summer 2020 terms. Undecided for Fall 2020. Accepts online lab coursework for Spring, Summer, and Fall 2020.

**Were tests required?** MCAT required.

**Are tests expected next year?** No, the Admissions Committee has decided to discontinue the GRE requirement for the class of 2026.

**What percent of admitted students participate in international experiences?** N/A

**What percent of current students take an extra year for research or a dual degree?** 17.1% dual degree. For more information on these programs, visit: https://vetmed.umn.edu/education-training/dvmphd-program

**What service learning opportunities exist?** Global One Health Initiative, Swine Program, and more. For more information, visit: https://vetmed.umn.edu/centers-programs

**NAVLE First-Time Pass Rate:** 96% (2020)

ILLINOIS

INDIANA

IOWA

KANSAS

MICHIGAN

MINNESOTA

MISSOURI

NEBRASKA

NORTH DAKOTA

OHIO

SOUTH DAKOTA

WISCONSIN

# MIDWEST

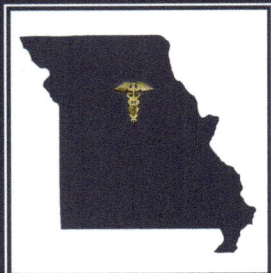

ILLINOIS

INDIANA

IOWA

KANSAS

MICHIGAN

MINNESOTA

MISSOURI

NEBRASKA

NORTH DAKOTA

OHIO

SOUTH DAKOTA

WISCONSIN

# UNIVERSITY OF MISSOURI - COLUMBIA
## COLLEGE OF VETERINARY MEDICINE

**Address:** 900 E Campus Dr, Columbia, MO 65211
**Website:** https://cvm.missouri.edu/
**Contact:** https://cvm.missouri.edu/prospective-students/contact-the-admissions-office/
**Phone:** (573) 882-3554

## COST OF ATTENDANCE

**In-State Tuition:** $27,840
**Fees & Expenses:** $20,608
**Total:** $48,448

**Out-of-State Tuition:** $65,170
**Fees & Expenses:** $21,432
**Total:** $86,602

**Financial Aid:** https://cvm.missouri.edu/financial-aid/financial-aid-overview/

## ADDITIONAL INFORMATION

**Interesting tidbit:** The Doctor of Veterinary Medicine professional program at the College of Veterinary Medicine boasts nearly two years of hands-on training in the college's general and specialty clinics. Preceptorships during the third and fourth years are supported by a new database system and a preceptor coordinator who ensures that each student is guided toward the opportunities that best match their individual interests.

**Important Updates due to COVID-19:** Accepts online coursework to fulfill prerequisite requirements for Spring, Summer and Fall 2020. Accepts pass/fail coursework to fulfill prerequisite requirements for spring 2020 and summer 2020 terms. Undecided for Fall 2020. Accepts online lab coursework for Spring, Summer and Fall 2020.

**Were tests required?** No.

**Are tests expected next year?** No.

**What percent of admitted students participate in international experiences?** N/A

**What percent of current students take an extra year for research or a dual degree?** 35% dual degree. For more information on this program, visit: https://healthprofessions.missouri.edu/mph/mphdvm-doctor-veterinary-medicine/

**What service learning opportunities exist?** Clinical training takes place at the Veterinary Health Center, treating 20,000 animals in the area and in local farms.

**NAVLE First-Time Pass Rate:** 97% (2020)

**Other:** Early Acceptance Program available for high school applicants. For more information, visit: https://cvm.missouri.edu/prospective-students/early-acceptance-programs/

# OHIO STATE UNIVERSITY COLLEGE OF VETERINARY MEDICINE

**Address:** 1900 Coffey Rd, Columbus, OH 43210
**Website:** https://vet.osu.edu/
**Contact:** https://vet.osu.edu/education/dvm/contact-us
**Phone:** (614) 292-1171

## COST OF ATTENDANCE

**In-State Tuition:** $33,587
**Fees & Expenses:** $22,133
**Total:** $55,720

**Out-of-State Tuition:** $72,923
**Fees & Expenses:** $22,133
**Total:** $95,056

**Financial Aid:** https://vet.osu.edu/education/professional-dvm-program-admissions/financial-aid-information

## ADDITIONAL INFORMATION

**Interesting tidbit:** OSU CVM treats more than 40,000 animal patients per year and has an animal blood bank that provides blood products to veterinary hospitals across America.

**Important Updates due to COVID-19:** Accept online coursework from accredited programs. accept all pass/fail coursework completed during the spring 2020 and summer 2020 semesters.

**Were tests required?** No.

**Are tests expected next year?** No.

**What percent of admitted students participate in international experiences?** N/A, Global Engagement available. For more information, visit: https://vet.osu.edu/departments-offices/global-engagement-program

**What percent of current students take an extra year for research or a dual degree?** 10.4% dual degree. For more information on these programs, visit: https://vet.osu.edu/education/graduate-programs/about-our-programs

**What service learning opportunities exist?** Several opportunities. For more information, visit: https://vet.osu.edu/departments-offices/global-engagement-program/opportunities#service%20learning

**NAVLE First-Time Pass Rate:** 97% (2020)

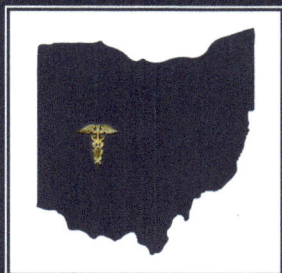

ILLINOIS

INDIANA

IOWA

KANSAS

MICHIGAN

MINNESOTA

MISSOURI

NEBRASKA

NORTH DAKOTA

OHIO

SOUTH DAKOTA

WISCONSIN

# MIDWEST

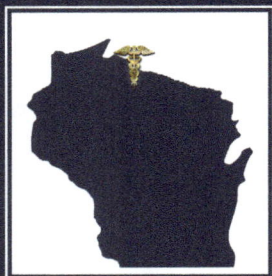

ILLINOIS

INDIANA

IOWA

KANSAS

MICHIGAN

MINNESOTA

MISSOURI

NEBRASKA

NORTH DAKOTA

OHIO

SOUTH DAKOTA

WISCONSIN

# UNIVERSITY OF WISCONSIN-MADISON SCHOOL OF VETERINARY MEDICINE

**Address:** 2015 Linden Dr., Madison, WI 53706
**Website:** https://www.vetmed.wisc.edu/
**Contact:** https://www.vetmed.wisc.edu/contact-us/
**Phone:** (608) 263-2525

## COST OF ATTENDANCE

**In-State Tuition:** $32,902
**Fees & Expenses:** $21,872
**Total:** $54,774

**Out-of-State Tuition:** $52,150
**Fees & Expenses:** $21,872
**Total:** $74,022

**Financial Aid:** https://www.vetmed.wisc.edu/education/dvm/awards-costs-aid/

## ADDITIONAL INFORMATION

**Interesting tidbit:** The School of Veterinary Medicine houses a veterinary medical teaching hospital, UW Veterinary Care. The school has an outstanding research program and many faculty members have joint appointments with the College of Agricultural and Life Sciences, the School of Medicine and Public Health, the Wisconsin National Primate Research Center, the McArdle Laboratory for Cancer Research, the National Wildlife Health Laboratory, and the North Central Dairy Forage Center.

**Important Updates due to COVID-19:** Accepts online coursework to fulfill prerequisite requirements. Accepts pass/fail coursework to fulfill prerequisite requirements. Accept online lab coursework.

**Were tests required?** No.

**Are tests expected next year?** No.

**What percent of admitted students participate in international experiences?** N/A

**What percent of current students take an extra year for research or a dual degree?** 11.5% dual degree. For more information on these programs, visit: https://www.vetmed.wisc.edu/education/dvm/dual-degree/. For more information on research experiences for admitted students, visit: https://www.vetmed.wisc.edu/research/dvm-student-research-experience/

**What service learning opportunities exist?** Shelter Medicine Program

**NAVLE First-Time Pass Rate:** 100% (2020)

**Other:** Food Animal Veterinary Medical Scholars available for qualified first-year undergraduate students. This program allows conditional acceptance to the DVM program. For more information: https://www.vetmed.wisc.edu/education/dvm/favemeds/

CHAPTER 4

# REGION THREE
# SOUTH

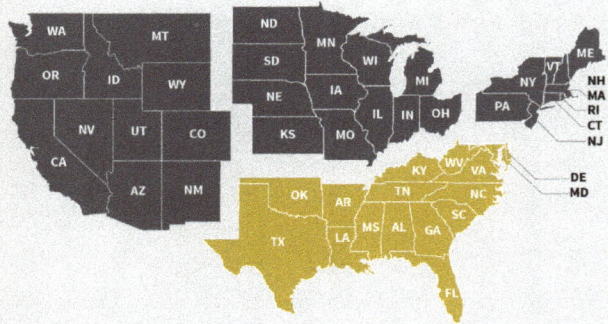

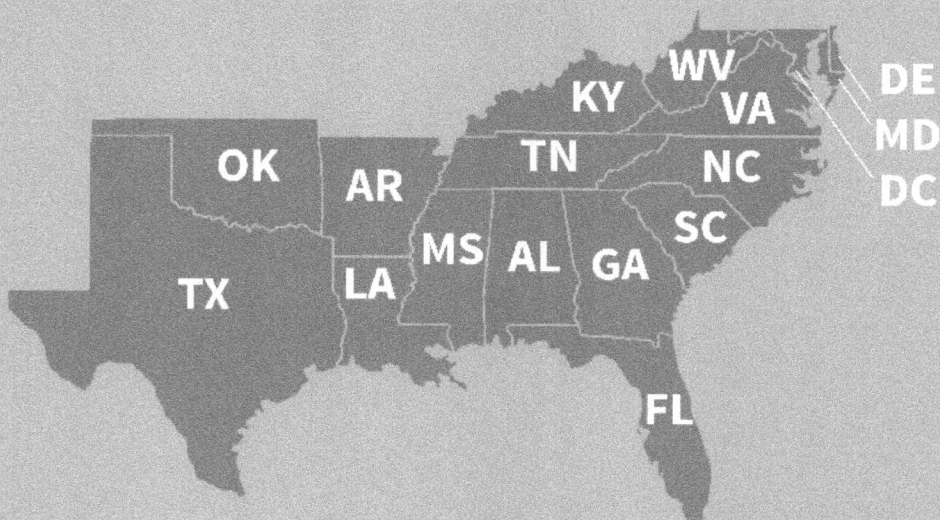

# 13 Programs | 16 States

1. AL – Auburn University College of Veterinary Medicine
2. AL – Tuskegee University School of Veterinary Medicine
3. FL – University of Florida College of Veterinary Medicine
4. GA – University of Georgia College of Veterinary Medicine
5. LA - Louisiana State University School of Veterinary Medicine
6. MS – Mississippi State University College of Veterinary Medicine
7. NC – North Carolina State University College of Veterinary Medicine
8. OK – Oklahoma State University College of Veterinary Medicine
9. TN – Lincoln Memorial University College of Veterinary Medicine
10. TN – University of Tennessee College of Veterinary Medicine
11. TX – Texas A&M University College of Veterinary Medicine & Biomedical Sciences
12. TX - Texas Tech University School of Veterinary Medicine
13. VA – Virginia Tech Virginia-Maryland College of Veterinary Medicine

# VETERINARY PROGRAMS

| Veterinary School | Avg. GPA & GRE<br><br>Early Decision (ED): Yes/No<br><br>Int'l Students: Yes/No<br><br>Reapps: Yes/No | Admissions Statistics | Science Req. Other than Gen Chem, OChem, Physics, Bio |
|---|---|---|---|
| **Auburn University**<br><br>1150 Wire Rd, Auburn, AL 36849 | 3.7 (overall)<br><br>GRE: 305<br><br>ED: No<br><br>Int'l Student: No<br><br>Reapps: N/A | **(2019)**<br>Apps Received: 900<br>Interview Received: 350<br>Number Enrolled: 130<br>Admitted Rate: 14.4%<br><br>**(2020)**<br>Apps Received: 1,032<br>Interview Received: 450<br>Number Enrolled: 130<br>Admitted Rate: 12.6% | Social/Behavioral Science<br>Pre-Calc/Trig or higher<br>Cell Biology<br>Biochemistry<br>Animal Nutrition<br>Science electives |
| **Tuskegee University**<br><br>1200 W. Montgomery Rd., Tuskegee, AL 36088 | 3.4 (overall)<br><br>GRE: 296<br><br>ED: No<br><br>Int'l Student: No<br><br>Reapps: Yes | **(2019)**<br>Apps Received: N/A<br>Interview Received: N/A<br>Number Enrolled: 66<br>Admitted Rate: N/A<br><br>**(2020)**<br>Apps Received: 268<br>Interview Received: 152<br>Number Enrolled: 56<br>Admitted Rate: 20.9% | Mathematics<br>Medical Terminology<br>Advanced Biol. Courses<br>Biochemistry w/ Lab<br>Science Electives<br>Intro to Animal Sciences |
| **University of Florida**<br><br>2015 SW 16th Ave, Gainesville, FL 32608 | 3.56 (overall)<br>3.47 (science)<br><br>GRE:<br>Not Required<br><br>ED: No<br><br>Int'l Student: Yes<br><br>Reapps: Yes | **(2019)**<br>Apps Received: 1,242<br>Interview Received: 325<br>Number Enrolled: 119<br>Admitted Rate: 9.58%<br><br>**(2020)**<br>Apps Received: 1,372<br>Interview Received: 386<br>Number Enrolled: 121<br>Admitted Rate: 8.82% | Microbio. w/ Lab<br>Genetics<br>Biochemistry<br>Statistics<br>Advanced Electives<br>Social Science/Humanit. |

# VETERINARY PROGRAMS

| Veterinary School | Avg. GPA & GRE<br><br>Early Decision (ED): Yes/No<br><br>Int'l Students: Yes/No<br><br>Reapps: Yes/No | Admissions Statistics | Science Req. Other than Gen Chem, OChem, Physics, Bio |
|---|---|---|---|
| **University of Georgia**<br><br>501 D. W. Brooks Dr., Athens, GA 30602 | 3.66 (overall)<br><br>GRE: 312<br><br>ED: No<br><br>Int'l Student: Yes<br><br>Reapps: Yes | **(2019)**<br>Apps Received: N/A<br>Interview Received: Not Required<br>Number Enrolled: 114<br>Admitted Rate: N/A<br><br>**(2020)**<br>Apps Received: 1,398<br>Interview Received: Not Required<br>Number Enrolled: 125<br>Admitted Rate: 8.94% | Biochemistry<br>Advanced Biol. (rec. comparative anatomy, physio., microbio., cell bio., or genetics) |
| **Louisiana State University**<br><br>Skip Bertman Dr., Baton Rouge, LA 70803 | 3.79 (science)<br><br>GRE: 306<br><br>ED: No<br><br>Int'l Student: Yes<br><br>Reapps: Yes | **(2019)**<br>Apps Received: 757<br>Interview Received: 400<br>Number Enrolled: 111<br>Admitted Rate: 14.7%<br><br>**(2020)**<br>Apps Received: 774<br>Interview Received: 102<br>Number Enrolled: 115<br>Admitted Rate: 14.9% | Microbiology<br>Biochemistry<br>College-level Math |
| **Mississippi State Univ.**<br><br>240 Wise Center Dr., Mississippi State, MS 39762 | 3.8 (overall)<br><br>GRE: Not Required<br><br>ED: No<br><br>Int'l Student: Yes<br><br>Reapps: N/A | **(2019)**<br>Apps Received: 1,200<br>Interview Received: N/A<br>Number Enrolled: 96<br>Admitted Rate: 8%<br><br>**(2020)**<br>Apps Received: 1,170<br>Interview Received: 321<br>Number Enrolled: 97<br>Admitted Rate: 8.3% | College-level Math<br>Microbio. w/ Lab<br>Biochemistry<br>Adv. Science Electives |

## SOUTH

# VETERINARY PROGRAMS

| Veterinary School | Avg. GPA & GRE<br><br>Early Decision (ED): Yes/No<br><br>Int'l Students: Yes/No<br><br>Reapps: Yes/No | Admissions Statistics | Science Req. Other than Gen Chem, OChem, Physics, Bio |
|---|---|---|---|
| **North Carolina State**<br><br>1060 William Moore Dr., Raleigh, NC 27606 | 3.71 (overall)<br>3.67 (science)<br><br>GRE:<br>Not Required<br><br>ED: No<br><br>Int'l Student: Yes<br><br>Reapps: N/A | **(2019)**<br>Apps Received: 1,219<br>Interview Received: Not Required<br>Number Enrolled: 100<br>Admitted Rate: 8.2%<br><br>**(2020)**<br>Apps Received: 1,156<br>Interview Received: Not Required<br>Number Enrolled: 100<br>Admitted Rate: 8.7% | Animal Nutrition<br>Biochemistry<br>Genetics<br>Social Sciences<br>Microbio. w/ Lab<br>Statistics |
| **Oklahoma State University**<br><br>208 N McFarland St, Stillwater, OK 74078 | 3.60 (overall)<br>3.59 (science)<br><br>GRE:<br>152 (V)<br>152 (Q)<br><br>ED: No<br><br>Int'l Student: Yes<br><br>Reapps: N/A | **(2019)**<br>Apps Received: 939<br>Interview Received: Only OK residents<br>Number Enrolled: 106<br>Admitted Rate: 11.3%<br><br>**(2020)**<br>Apps Received: 917<br>Interview Received: 107 (OK residents only)<br>Number Enrolled: 72<br>Admitted Rate: 6.0% | Biochemistry<br>Statistics<br>Animal Nutrition |
| **Lincoln Memorial University**<br><br>6965 Cumberland Gap Pkwy, Harrogate, TN 37752 | 3.4 (overall)<br>3.2 (science)<br><br>GRE:<br>Not Required<br><br>ED: No<br><br>Int'l Student: Yes<br><br>Reapps: Yes | **(2019)**<br>Apps Received: 1,400<br>Interview Received: N/A<br>Number Enrolled: 125<br>Admitted Rate: 8.9%<br><br>**(2020)**<br>Apps Received: 1,880<br>Interview Received: 620<br>Number Enrolled: 125<br>Admitted Rate: 6.7% | Genetics<br>Biochemistry<br>Adv. Science Electives<br>Social Sciences |

# VETERINARY PROGRAMS

| Veterinary School | Avg. GPA & GRE / Early Decision (ED): Yes/No / Int'l Students: Yes/No / Reapps: Yes/No | Admissions Statistics | Science Req. Other than Gen Chem, OChem, Physics, Bio |
|---|---|---|---|
| **University of Tennessee**<br><br>2407 River Dr., Knoxville, TN 37996 | 3.61 (overall)<br><br>GRE:<br>Not Required<br><br>ED: No<br><br>Int'l Student: Yes<br><br>Reapps: Yes | **(2019)**<br>Apps Received: 1,067<br>Interview Received: 401<br>Number Enrolled: 85<br>Admitted Rate: 7.9%<br><br>**(2020)**<br>Apps Received: 1,067<br>Interview Received: 410<br>Number Enrolled: 85<br>Admitted Rate: 8.0% | Social Sciences<br>Cellular Biology<br>Genetics<br>Biochemistry |
| **Texas A&M University**<br><br>4461 TAMU, College Station, TX 77843 | 3.72 (overall)<br><br>GRE:<br>Not Required<br><br>ED: No<br><br>Int'l Student: No<br><br>Reapps: N/A | **(2019)**<br>Apps Received: 509 ('17)<br>Interview Received: 219<br>Number Enrolled: 162<br>Admitted Rate: 26.7%<br><br>**(2020)**<br>Apps Received: 676<br>Interview Received: 253<br>Number Enrolled: 162<br>Admitted Rate: 24.0% | Microbio. w/ Lab<br>Genetics<br>Animal Nutrition or Feeds & Feeding<br>Biochemistry<br>Statistics |
| **Texas Tech University**<br><br>7671 Evan Dr., Amarillo, TX 79106 | 2.9+ (overall)<br>2.9+ (science)<br><br>GRE:<br>Not Required.<br><br>ED: No<br><br>Int'l Student: No<br><br>Reapps: N/A | **(2019)**<br>N/A<br><br>**(2020)***<br>Apps Received: N/A<br>Interview Received: N/A<br>Number Enrolled: N/A<br>Admitted Rate: N/A<br><br>*Inaugural class matriculates in Fall 2021. | Animal Nutrition<br>Biochemistry<br>English<br>Genetics<br>Microbiology<br>Statistics |

## SOUTH

# VETERINARY PROGRAMS

| Veterinary School | Avg. GPA & GRE<br><br>Early Decision (ED): Yes/No<br><br>Int'l Students: Yes/No<br><br>Reapps: Yes/No | Admissions Statistics | Science Req. Other than Gen Chem, OChem, Physics, Bio |
|---|---|---|---|
| **Virginia Tech**<br><br>205 Duck Pond Dr., Blacksburg, VA 24060 | 3.55 (overall)<br>3.51 (science)<br><br>GRE:<br>Not Required<br><br>ED: No<br><br>Int'l Student: Yes<br><br>Reapps: N/A | **(2019)**<br>Apps Received: 1,832<br>Interview Received: N/A<br>Number Enrolled: 126<br>Admitted Rate: 6.9%<br><br>**(2020)**<br>Apps Received: 1,461<br>Interview Received: 320<br>Number Enrolled: 127<br>Admitted Rate:8.7% | Biochemistry<br>Math<br>Social Sciences<br>Medical Terminology |

ALABAMA

ARKANSAS

DELAWARE

DISTRICT OF
COLUMBIA

FLORIDA

GEORGIA

KENTUCKY

LOUISIANA

MARYLAND

MISSISSIPPI

NORTH CAROLINA

OKLAHOMA

SOUTH CAROLINA

TENNESSEE

TEXAS

VIRGINIA

WEST VIRGINIA

# AUBURN UNIVERSITY COLLEGE OF VETERINARY MEDICINE

**Address:** 1150 Wire Rd, Auburn, AL 36849
**Website:** *https://www.vetmed.auburn.edu/*
**Email:** *admissions@vetmed.auburn.edu*
**Phone:** (334) 844-2685

## COST OF ATTENDANCE

**In-State Tuition:** $22,880
**Fees & Expenses:** $23,011
**Total:** $45,891

**Out-of-State Tuition:** $49,040
**Fees & Expenses:** $23,011
**Total:** $72,051

**Financial Aid:** Submit FAFSA to be considered for any financial aid. Scholarships available annually to students after the first semester. For more information, contact admissions.

## ADDITIONAL INFORMATION

**Interesting tidbit:** Auburn was a part of the first regional education program in the U.S., offering veterinary education programs to eight neighboring states. Auburn is particularly proud of its continuous 69-year partnership in veterinary education with the Commonwealth of Kentucky through the Southern Regional Education Board. That is why Kentucky residents pay in-state tuition at Auburn University CVM.

**Important Updates due to COVID-19:** Accept pass and satisfactory grades from incoming students or applicants whose institutions have transitioned to pass/fail, satisfactory/unsatisfactory, or other grading practices for the spring 2020/summer 2020 terms.

**Were tests required?** No, GRE requirement waived for Class of 2025 (2020-21 application cycle).

**Are tests expected next year?** Yes.

**What percent of admitted students participate in international experiences?** N/A

**What percent of current students take an extra year for research or a dual degree?** 10% dual degree. For more information on these programs, visit: https://www.vetmed.auburn.edu/education/dual-degree-programs/

**What service learning opportunities exist?** Southeastern Raptor Center: DVM students and undergraduates gain hands-on experience in rehabilitating local wild raptors.

**NAVLE First-Time Pass Rate:** 97% (2020)

# TUSKEGEE UNIVERSITY SCHOOL OF VETERINARY MEDICINE

**Address:** 1200 W. Montgomery Rd., Tuskegee, AL 36088
**Website:** *https://www.tuskegee.edu/programs-courses/colleges-schools/cvm*
**Contact:** *https://www.tuskegee.edu/programs-courses/colleges-schools/cvm/cvm-contacts*
**Phone:** (334) 727-8174

## COST OF ATTENDANCE

**Tuition:** $41,170
**Fees & Expenses:** $3,020*
**Total:** $44,190

*Fees reflect only the mandatory fees. Indirect costs information is unavailable.

**Financial Aid:** https://www.tuskegee.edu/programs-courses/colleges-schools/cvm/tucvm-scholarships

## ADDITIONAL INFORMATION

**Interesting tidbit:** The Tuskegee University College of Veterinary Medicine (TUCVM) is the only veterinary medical professional program located on the campus of a historically black college or university (HBCU) in the United States. The TUCVM has educated more than 70 percent of the nation's African-American veterinarians.

**Important Updates due to COVID-19:** Accepts online coursework to fulfill prerequisite requirements. Accepts pass/fail coursework to fulfill prerequisite requirements. Accept online lab coursework.

**Were tests required?** GRE required.

**Are tests expected next year?** Yes.

**What percent of admitted students participate in international experiences?** N/A

**What percent of current students take an extra year for research or a dual degree?** N/A

**What service learning opportunities exist?** Shelter Medicine Program

**NAVLE First-Time Pass Rate:** 81% (2019)

ALABAMA
ARKANSAS
DELAWARE
DISTRICT OF COLUMBIA
FLORIDA
GEORGIA
KENTUCKY
LOUISIANA
MARYLAND
MISSISSIPPI
NORTH CAROLINA
OKLAHOMA
SOUTH CAROLINA
TENNESSEE
TEXAS
VIRGINIA
WEST VIRGINIA

# SOUTH

ALABAMA

ARKANSAS

DELAWARE

DISTRICT OF COLUMBIA

FLORIDA

GEORGIA

KENTUCKY

LOUISIANA

MARYLAND

MISSISSIPPI

NORTH CAROLINA

OKLAHOMA

SOUTH CAROLINA

TENNESSEE

TEXAS

VIRGINIA

WEST VIRGINIA

# UNIVERSITY OF FLORIDA COLLEGE OF VETERINARY MEDICINE

**Address:** 2015 SW 16th Ave, Gainesville, FL 32608
**Website:** *https://education.vetmed.ufl.edu/*
**Contact:** *https://education.vetmed.ufl.edu/about-us/*
**Phone:** (352) 294-4203

## COST OF ATTENDANCE

**In-State Tuition:** $28,790
**Fees & Expenses:** $19,562
**Total:** $48,352

**Out-of-State Tuition:** $45,500
**Fees & Expenses:** $24,400
**Total:** $64,062

**Financial Aid:** https://education.vetmed.ufl.edu/admissions/financial-aid-information/

## ADDITIONAL INFORMATION

**Interesting tidbit:** The College of Veterinary Medicine is part of the Institute of Food and Agricultural Sciences and a member of the UF Health Science Center, home to physicians, dentists, veterinarians, and clinical and research scientists.

**Important Updates due to COVID-19:** Accepts online coursework to fulfill prerequisite requirements for Spring, Summer, and Fall 2020. Accepts pass/fail coursework to fulfill prerequisite requirements for Spring/Summer 2020 (not Fall 2020) if this is the only option offered to the student. Accepts online lab coursework for Spring, Summer, and Fall 2020.

**Were tests required?** No.

**Are tests expected next year?** No.

**What percent of admitted students participate in international experiences?** N/A, international externships available. For more information, visit: https://education.vetmed.ufl.edu/dvm-curriculum/externships/

**What percent of current students take an extra year for research or a dual degree?** N/A, dual degree options available: https://education.vetmed.ufl.edu/admissions/dvmmph-joint-degree-program/

**What service learning opportunities exist?** Certificate in Shelter Medicine

**NAVLE First-Time Pass Rate:** 96% (2020)

**Other:** Online Master's degree and courses in Shelter Medicine available.

# UNIVERSITY OF GEORGIA COLLEGE OF VETERINARY MEDICINE

**Address:** 501 D. W. Brooks Drive, Athens, GA 30602
**Website:** *https://vet.uga.edu/*
**Contact:** *https://vet.uga.edu/location/main-campus-cvm/*
**Phone:** (706) 542-4979

## COST OF ATTENDANCE

**In-State Tuition:** $17,514
**Fees & Expenses:** $19,876
**Total:** $37,390

**Out-of-State Tuition:** $47,176
**Fees & Expenses:** $20,522
**Total:** $67,698

**Financial Aid:** https://vet.uga.edu/education/dvm-program/tuition-and-fees/

## ADDITIONAL INFORMATION

**Interesting tidbit:** DVM students may apply for the Specialty Focus designation in the spring of their second year.  The Specialty Focus designation provides students who have unique career interests in Poultry, Clinical and Anatomic Pathology, Zoological/Wildlife/Conservation Medicine, Laboratory Animal Medicine, or Public Health with six additional weeks of externship time (in addition to the standard maximum of 12 weeks) during their clinical year.

**Important Updates due to COVID-19:** Accepts online coursework to fulfill prerequisite requirements. Accepts pass/fail coursework to fulfill prerequisite requirements. Accept online lab coursework.

**Were tests required?** GRE required.

**Are tests expected next year?** Yes.

**What percent of admitted students participate in international experiences?** N/A, IVM Certificate Available. For more information, visit: https://vet.uga.edu/education/dvm-program/dvm-international-program/

**What percent of current students take an extra year for research or a dual degree?** 19.3% dual degree. For more information on these programs, visit: https://vet.uga.edu/education/phd-and-masters-degree-programs/ . Research opportunities available for DVM students. For more information, visit: https://vet.uga.edu/research/student-research-opportunities/

**What service learning opportunities exist?**  Variety of Service Labs. For more information, visit: https://vet.uga.edu/diagnostic-service-labs/

**NAVLE First-Time Pass Rate:** 95% (2020)

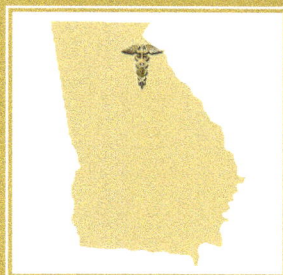

ALABAMA
ARKANSAS
DELAWARE
DISTRICT OF COLUMBIA
FLORIDA
GEORGIA
KENTUCKY
LOUISIANA
MARYLAND
MISSISSIPPI
NORTH CAROLINA
OKLAHOMA
SOUTH CAROLINA
TENNESSEE
TEXAS
VIRGINIA
WEST VIRGINIA

OK AR TN KY WV VA NC SC D M D
TX LA MS AL GA
FL

# SOUTH

ALABAMA

ARKANSAS

DELAWARE

DISTRICT OF
COLUMBIA

FLORIDA

GEORGIA

KENTUCKY

LOUISIANA

MARYLAND

MISSISSIPPI

NORTH CAROLINA

OKLAHOMA

SOUTH CAROLINA

TENNESSEE

TEXAS

VIRGINIA

WEST VIRGINIA

# LOUISIANA STATE UNIVERSITY SCHOOL OF VETERINARY MEDICINE

**Address:** Skip Bertman Dr., Baton Rouge, LA 70803
**Website:** *https://www.lsu.edu/vetmed/*
**Contact:** *https://www.lsu.edu/vetmed/about_svm/contact_us.php*
**Phone:** (225) 578-9900

## COST OF ATTENDANCE

**In-State Tuition:** $24,128
**Fees & Expenses:** $29,515
**Total:** $53,643

**Out-of-State Tuition:** $53,228
**Fees & Expenses:** $29,515
**Total:** $82,743

**Financial Aid:** https://www.lsu.edu/financialaid/apply_for_aid/

## ADDITIONAL INFORMATION

**Interesting tidbit:** LSU SVM participates in the Southern Regional Education Board's program for education in veterinary medicine. Training contracts provide a limited number of entering spaces for qualified candidates from Arkansas.

**Important Updates due to COVID-19:** Accepts online coursework to fulfill prerequisite requirements. Accepts pass/fail coursework to fulfill prerequisite requirements. Accept online lab coursework.

**Were tests required?** No, GRE requirement waived for 2020/2021 application cycle.

**Are tests expected next year?** GRE required.

**What percent of admitted students participate in international experiences?** N/A

**What percent of current students take an extra year for research or a dual degree?** 4.4% dual degree. For more information on these programs, visit: https://www.lsu.edu/vetmed/dvm_admissions/other_applications/dvm_phd.php

**What service learning opportunities exist?** Shelter Medicine Support

**NAVLE First-Time Pass Rate:** 94% (2020)

# MISSISSIPPI STATE UNIVERSITY COLLEGE OF VETERINARY MEDICINE

**Address:** 240 Wise Center Drive, Mississippi State, MS 39762
**Website:** *https://www.vetmed.msstate.edu/*
**Contact:** *https://www.msstate.edu/directory*
**Phone:** (662) 325-3432

## COST OF ATTENDANCE

**In-State Tuition:** $27,248
**Fees & Expenses:** $20,970
**Total:** $48,218

**Out-of-State Tuition:** $48,448
**Fees & Expenses:** $20,970
**Total:** $69,418

**Financial Aid:** https://www.vetmed.msstate.edu/alumni-friends/opportunities-for-giving#scholarships

## ADDITIONAL INFORMATION

**Interesting tidbit:** MSU CVM is one of only a few colleges of veterinary medicine that—like most colleges of human medicine—requires two full years of mentored clinical education in addition to two years of pre-clinical (classroom and laboratory) coursework, whereas majority of CVM requires three years of pre-clinical and one year of clinical rotations.

**Important Updates due to COVID-19:** Accept all satisfactory and passing grades for prerequisite classes taken only during the spring 2020 term.

**Were tests required?** No.

**Are tests expected next year?** No.

**What percent of admitted students participate in international experiences?** N/A, International opportunities available. For more information, visit: https://www.vetmed.msstate.edu/academics/international-programs

**What percent of current students take an extra year for research or a dual degree?** 11.5% dual degree. For more information on these programs, visit: https://www.vetmed.msstate.edu/research/research-graduate-studies/research-programs

**What service learning opportunities exist?** Safe Haven for Pets, Homeward Bound, Animals in Focus, Shelter Medicine, and Vets for Vets. For more information on these opportunities, visit: https://www.vetmed.msstate.edu/outreach/community-engagement/service

**NAVLE First-Time Pass Rate:** 97% (2020)

**Other:** Early Entry Program available for high school applicants. For more information, visit: https://www.vetmed.msstate.edu/academics/early-entry-program

ALABAMA
ARKANSAS
DELAWARE
DISTRICT OF COLUMBIA
FLORIDA
GEORGIA
KENTUCKY
LOUISIANA
MARYLAND
MISSISSIPPI
NORTH CAROLINA
OKLAHOMA
SOUTH CAROLINA
TENNESSEE
TEXAS
VIRGINIA
WEST VIRGINIA

# SOUTH

# NORTH CAROLINA STATE UNIVERSITY COLLEGE OF VETERINARY MEDICINE

**Address:** 1060 William Moore Dr., Raleigh, NC 27606
**Website:** *https://cvm.ncsu.edu/*
**Contact:** *https://cvm.ncsu.edu/directory/?deptlisting=1*
**Phone:** (919) 513-6461

## COST OF ATTENDANCE

**In-State Tuition:** $19,616
**Fee & Expenses:** $19,953
**Total:** $39,569

**Out-of-State Tuition:** $47,657
**Fees & Expenses:** $19,953
**Total:** $67,610

**Financial Aid:** https://cvm.ncsu.edu/education/dvm/admission/costs/

## ADDITIONAL INFORMATION

**Interesting tidbit:** The clinical program at NC State Veterinary Medicine provides an opportunity for students to select "focus areas" to increase their depth of training in their intended area of post-graduate activity, while still retaining a broad-based veterinary education.

**Important Updates due to COVID-19:** Allow a Pass in P/F or Satisfactory in the S/U grading systems for prerequisites completed in Spring or Summer 2020. For Fall 2020, P/F and S/U accepted if it's the only option at the institution.

Were tests required? GRE required.

**Are tests expected next year?** No, NC State removed the GRE as a requirement for admission into the DVM program, starting with the 2021 admissions cycle.

**What percent of admitted students participate in international experiences?** N/A, Global health training: https://globalhealth.cvm.ncsu.edu/training/

**What percent of current students take an extra year for research or a dual degree?** 11% dual degree. For more information on these programs, visit: https://cvm.ncsu.edu/education/dvm/combined-degree-programs/

**What service learning opportunities exist?** Outreach programs admitted students may be interested in getting involved with: https://cvm.ncsu.edu/outreach/

**NAVLE First-Time Pass Rate:** 93% (2019)

**Other:** NCU CVM has a Teaching Animal Unit (TAU), an on-campus teaching lab for students to learn about procedures in livestock production.

ALABAMA

ARKANSAS

DELAWARE

DISTRICT OF COLUMBIA

FLORIDA

GEORGIA

KENTUCKY

LOUISIANA

MARYLAND

MISSISSIPPI

NORTH CAROLINA

OKLAHOMA

SOUTH CAROLINA

TENNESSEE

TEXAS

VIRGINIA

WEST VIRGINIA

# OKLAHOMA STATE UNIVERSITY COLLEGE OF VETERINARY MEDICINE

**Address:** 208 N McFarland St, Stillwater, OK 74078
**Website:** *https://vetmed.okstate.edu/*
**Contact:** *https://vetmed.okstate.edu/contact-us/index.html*
**Phone:** (405) 744-6961

## COST OF ATTENDANCE

**In-State Tuition:** $24,430
**Fees & Expenses:** $27,940
**Total:** $48,375

**Out-of-State Tuition:** $46,795
**Fees & Expenses:** $27,940
**Total:** $74,735

**Financial Aid:** https://vetmed.okstate.edu/students/expenses-and-financial-aid.html

## ADDITIONAL INFORMATION

**Interesting tidbit:** In the last five years, OSU-CVM faculty generated 569 publications, of which 11% were among the top 10% cited papers worldwide and 30.5 % were in the top 10 percent most frequently cited journals.

**Important Updates due to COVID-19:** Accept courses taken in the Pass/No Pass format for the Spring of 2020 semester, including prerequisite coursework.

**Were tests required?** GRE and CASPer required.

**Are tests expected next year?** Yes.

**What percent of admitted students participate in international experiences?** N/A

**What percent of current students take an extra year for research or a dual degree?** 7.5% dual degree. For more information on these programs, visit: https://vetmed.okstate.edu/students/dual-graduate-professional-programs.html

**What service learning opportunities exist?** Shelter Surgery rotation. For more information, visit: https://vetmed.okstate.edu/veterinary-medical-hospital/shelter-surgery.html

**NAVLE First-Time Pass Rate:** 100% (2019)

**Other:** Early Admission Program for first-year OK undergraduate students. For more information, visit: https://vetmed.okstate.edu/students/early-admission.html

ALABAMA
ARKANSAS
DELAWARE
DISTRICT OF COLUMBIA
FLORIDA
GEORGIA
KENTUCKY
LOUISIANA
MARYLAND
MISSISSIPPI
NORTH CAROLINA
OKLAHOMA
SOUTH CAROLINA
TENNESSEE
TEXAS
VIRGINIA
WEST VIRGINIA

# SOUTH

ALABAMA

ARKANSAS

DELAWARE

DISTRICT OF
COLUMBIA

FLORIDA

GEORGIA

KENTUCKY

LOUISIANA

MARYLAND

MISSISSIPPI

NORTH CAROLINA

OKLAHOMA

SOUTH CAROLINA

TENNESSEE

TEXAS

VIRGINIA

WEST VIRGINIA

# LINCOLN MEMORIAL UNIVERSITY COLLEGE OF VETERINARY MEDICINE

**Address:** 6965 Cumberland Gap Parkway, Harrogate, TN 37752
**Website:** *https://www.lmunet.edu/college-of-veterinary-medicine/index.php*
**Contact:** *https://www.lmunet.edu/college-of-veterinary-medicine/admissions/contact-us.php*
**Phone:** (423) 869-3611

## COST OF ATTENDANCE

**Tuition:** $50,500
**Fees &Expenses:** $21,114
**Total:** $71,614

**Financial Aid:** https://www.lmunet.edu/college-of-veterinary-medicine/admissions/financial-aid/scholarships.php

## ADDITIONAL INFORMATION

**Interesting tidbit:** Clinical Year Hybrid Distributive Education program prepares students by providing experience working in both primary care and specialty private practice environments. The large animal component of the DVTC provides a working farm environment with a large cattle and horse herd.

**Important Updates due to COVID-19:** For the Spring 2020 semester, Pass or Satisfactory will be accepted as an exception for course prerequisites requiring a grade of C- or higher. Pass or satisfactory is not accepted for any other semester or quarter at this time.

**Were tests required?** CASPer required.

**Are tests expected next year?** Yes.

**What percent of admitted students participate in international experiences?** N/A

**What percent of current students take an extra year for research or a dual degree?** N/A, DVM/MBA program available. Student research opportunities available: https://www.lmunet.edu/college-of-veterinary-medicine/research/student-opportunities/index.php

**Percent of admitted students who participated in research projects prior to matriculation:** approximately 50%

**What service learning opportunities exist?** Shelter Outreach to the Appalachian Region (SOAR) program.

**NAVLE First-Time Pass Rate:** 97% (2019/20)

**Other:** LMU-CVM is currently expanding its dual degree program offerings.

# UNIVERSITY OF TENNESSEE COLLEGE OF VETERINARY MEDICINE

**Address:** 2407 River Dr., Knoxville, TN 37996
**Website:** *https://vetmed.tennessee.edu/*
**Contact:** *https://vetmed.tennessee.edu/home/Pages/Contact-UTCVM.aspx*
**Phone:** (865) 974-8387

## COST OF ATTENDANCE

**In-State Tuition:** $29,336
**Fees & Expenses:** $23,086
**Total:** $52,422

**Out-of-State Tuition:** $56,602
**Fees & Expenses:** $23,086
**Total:** $79,688

**Financial Aid:** https://onestop.utk.edu/financial-aid/apply/

## ADDITIONAL INFORMATION

**Interesting tidbit:** In the fourth year, students participate exclusively in clinical rotations in the Veterinary Medical Center, satellite centers, and in up to 16 weeks of required off-campus externships. The clinical program does not include a specific tracking curriculum, but allows students to develop individual areas of focus based on their interest and career aspirations.

**Important Updates due to COVID-19:** For Spring, Summer and Fall 2020, accept online coursework and pass/fail coursework to fulfill prerequisite requirements and online lab coursework.

**Were tests required?** No, GRE requirement is temporarily suspended due to Covid-19.

**Are tests expected next year?** No.

**What percent of admitted students participate in international experiences?** N/A, Belize Zoo Rotation and other opportunities. For more information, visit: https://vetmed.tennessee.edu/academics/Pages/international.aspx

**What percent of current students take an extra year for research or a dual degree?** 22.5% dual degree. For more information on these programs, visit: https://vetmed.tennessee.edu/research/Pages/Graduate_Program.aspx

**What service learning opportunities exist?** Human-Animal Bond in Tennessee (HABIT), Companion Animal Initiative of Tennessee (CAIT), and Shelter Medicine programs available. For more information, visit: https://vetmed.tennessee.edu/outreach/Pages/default.aspx

**NAVLE First-Time Pass Rate:** 97% (2020)

ALABAMA
ARKANSAS
DELAWARE
DISTRICT OF COLUMBIA
FLORIDA
GEORGIA
KENTUCKY
LOUISIANA
MARYLAND
MISSISSIPPI
NORTH CAROLINA
OKLAHOMA
SOUTH CAROLINA
TENNESSEE
TEXAS
VIRGINIA
WEST VIRGINIA

# SOUTH

ALABAMA

ARKANSAS

DELAWARE

DISTRICT OF
COLUMBIA

FLORIDA

GEORGIA

KENTUCKY

LOUISIANA

MARYLAND

MISSISSIPPI

NORTH CAROLINA

OKLAHOMA

SOUTH CAROLINA

TENNESSEE

TEXAS

VIRGINIA

WEST VIRGINIA

# TEXAS A&M UNIVERSITY COLLEGE OF VETERINARY MEDICINE & BIOMEDICAL SCIENCES

**Address:** 4461 TAMU, College Station, TX 77843
**Website:** *https://vetmed.tamu.edu/*
**Contact:** *https://vetmed.tamu.edu/stevenson-center/contact-us/*
**Phone:** (979) 862-1169

## COST OF ATTENDANCE

**In-State Tuition:** $26,320
**Fee & Expenses:** $20,290
**Total:** $46,610

**Out-of-State Tuition:** $42,022
**Fees & Expenses:** $21,560
**Total:** $63,582

**Financial Aid:** Students are encouraged to apply for federal financial aid.

## ADDITIONAL INFORMATION

**Interesting tidbit:** The DVM Professional Program at the Texas A&M College of Veterinary Medicine & Biomedical Sciences (CVMBS) is one of the oldest and most prestigious programs of its kind in the United States. In the fourth year of the program, students spend 12 months on clinical rotations in the VMTH and other venues, including the Houston SPCA, the Texas Department of Criminal Justice (TDCJ), and externship experiences at locations of the student's choice.

**Important Updates due to COVID-19:** Accepts online coursework to fulfill prerequisite requirements. Accepts pass/fail coursework to fulfill prerequisite requirements. Accept online lab coursework.

**Were tests required?** Altus Suite required.

**Are tests expected next year?** Yes.

**What percent of admitted students participate in international experiences?** N/A, International programs available. For more information, visit: https://vetmed.tamu.edu/international-programs/

**What percent of current students take an extra year for research or a dual degree?** 3.1% dual degree.

**What service learning opportunities exist?** Global Outreach and research opportunities available. For more information, visit: https://onehealth.tamu.edu/outreach/

**NAVLE First-Time Pass Rate:** 98% (2019)

# TEXAS TECH UNIVERSITY SCHOOL OF VETERINARY MEDICINE

**Address:** 7671 Evans Drive, Amarillo, TX 79106
**Website:** *https://www.depts.ttu.edu/vetschool/*
**Contact:** *https://www.depts.ttu.edu/vetschool/contact-us/*
**Phone:** (806) 742-2011

## COST OF ATTENDANCE

**In-State Tuition:** $22,000
**Fee & Expenses:** $19,790
**Total:** $41,790

**Out-of-State Tuition:** $32,800
**Fees & Expenses:** $19,790
**Total:** $52,590

**Financial Aid:** https://www.depts.ttu.edu/financialaid/

## ADDITIONAL INFORMATION

**Interesting tidbit:** The TTU SVM will welcome its inaugural class in Fall 2021. Applicants must be residents of Texas or New Mexico. Less than 10% of the class will consist of New Mexico residents.

**Important Updates due to COVID-19:** N/A

**Were tests required?** CASPer required.

**Are tests expected next year?** Yes.

**What percent of admitted students participate in international experiences?** N/A

**What percent of current students take an extra year for research or a dual degree?** N/A

**What service learning opportunities exist?** N/A

**NAVLE First-Time Pass Rate:** N/A

ALABAMA
ARKANSAS
DELAWARE
DISTRICT OF COLUMBIA
FLORIDA
GEORGIA
KENTUCKY
LOUISIANA
MARYLAND
MISSISSIPPI
NORTH CAROLINA
OKLAHOMA
SOUTH CAROLINA
TENNESSEE
TEXAS
VIRGINIA
WEST VIRGINIA

# SOUTH

ALABAMA

ARKANSAS

DELAWARE

DISTRICT OF
COLUMBIA

FLORIDA

GEORGIA

KENTUCKY

LOUISIANA

MARYLAND

MISSISSIPPI

NORTH CAROLINA

OKLAHOMA

SOUTH CAROLINA

TENNESSEE

TEXAS

VIRGINIA

WEST VIRGINIA

# VIRGINIA TECH VIRGINIA-MARYLAND COLLEGE OF VETERINARY MEDICINE

**Address:** 205 Duck Pond Dr., Blacksburg, VA 24060
**Website:** *http://www.vetmed.vt.edu/*
**Contact:** *http://becomeaveterinarian.vetmed.vt.edu/inquiryform*
**Phone:** (540) 231-7666

## COST OF ATTENDANCE

**In-State Tuition:** $22,540
**Fees & Expenses:** $24,510
**Total:** $47,050

**Out-of-State Tuition:** $51,900
**Fees & Expenses:** $25,620
**Total:** $77,520

*VA and MD residents pay in-state tuition.

**Financial Aid:** https://finaid.vt.edu/graduate-students/special-groups/vet-med.html

## ADDITIONAL INFORMATION

**Interesting tidbit:** The college's locations include the main campus in Blacksburg, Virginia; the Animal Cancer Care and Research Center in Roanoke, Virginia; the Marion duPont Scott Equine Medical Center in Leesburg, Virginia; and the Gudelsky Veterinary Center in College Park, Maryland.

**Important Updates due to COVID-19:** Accept online coursework from accredited programs. Accept all pass/fail coursework completed during the spring 2020 and summer 2020 semesters. Accept no more than 50 percent of pass/fail coursework.

**Were tests required?** No.

**Are tests expected next year?** No.

**What percent of admitted students participate in international experiences?** N/A, International activities available. For more information, visit: http://www.vetmed.vt.edu/international/

**What percent of current students take an extra year for research or a dual degree?** 23.6% dual degree. For more information on this program, visit: https://bmvs.vetmed.vt.edu/

**What service learning opportunities exist?** Center for Animal Human Relationships (CENTAUR): http://www.vetmed.vt.edu/centaur/

**NAVLE First-Time Pass Rate:** 93% (2020)

ALASKA

ARIZONA

CALIFORNIA

COLORADO

HAWAII

IDAHO

MONTANA

NEVADA

NEW MEXICO

OREGON

UTAH

WASHINGTON

WYOMING

CHAPTER 5

## REGION FOUR

# WEST

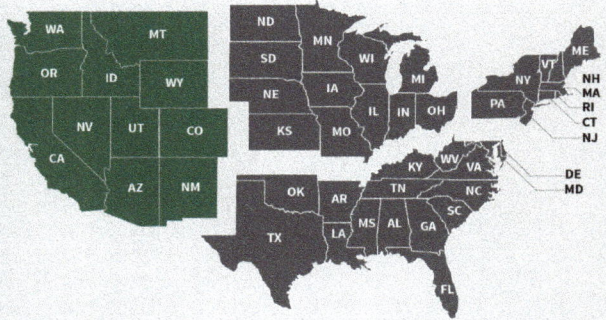

# 7 Programs | 13 States

1. AZ – Midwestern University College of Veterinary Medicine
2. AZ - University of Arizona College of Veterinary Medicine
3. CA – University of California, Davis School of Veterinary Medicine
4. CA – Western University of Health Sciences
5. CO – Colorado State University College of Veterinary Medicine and Biomedical Sciences
6. OR – Oregon State University College of Veterinary Medicine
7. WA - Washington State University College of Veterinary Medicine

| Veterinary School | Avg. GPA & GRE<br><br>Early Decision (ED): Yes/No<br><br>Int'l Students: Yes/No<br><br>Reapps: Yes/No | Admissions Statistics | Science Req. Other than Gen Chem, OChem, Physics, Bio |
|---|---|---|---|
| **Midwestern University**<br><br>19555 N 59th Ave., Glendale, AZ 85308 | 3.56 (overall)<br><br>GRE:<br>Not Required<br><br>ED: No<br><br>Int'l Student: Yes<br><br>Reapps: Yes | **(2019)**<br>Apps Received: N/A<br>Interview Received: N/A<br>Number Enrolled: 129<br>Admitted Rate: N/A<br><br>**(2020)**<br>Apps Received: 1,344<br>Interview Received: 413<br>Number Enrolled: 125<br>Admitted Rate: 9.3% | Biochemistry<br>Mathematics<br>Science Electives |
| **University of Arizona**<br><br>1580 E Hanley Blvd., Oro Valley, AZ 85737 | 3.0+ (overall)<br>3.0+ (science)<br><br>GRE:<br>Not Required<br><br>ED: No<br><br>Int'l Student: Yes<br><br>Reapps: Yes | **(2019)**<br>N/A<br><br>**(2020)**<br>Apps Received: 518<br>Interview Received: 270<br>Number Enrolled: 100<br>Admitted Rate: 19.3% | Biochemistry<br>Mathematics<br>English Composition<br>Arts & Humanities<br>Social Sciences |
| **UC Davis**<br><br>1 Garrod Dr., Davis, CA 95616 | Resident:<br>3.7 (science)<br><br>Non-resident:<br>3.96 (science)<br><br>GRE:<br>68% (Q; Resident)<br>82% (Q; Non-resident)<br><br>ED: No<br><br>Int'l Student: Yes<br><br>Reapps: Yes | **(2019)**<br>Apps Received: 979<br>Interview Received: 180<br>Number Enrolled: 147<br>Admitted Rate: 15.0%<br><br>**(2020)**<br>Apps Received: 1,012<br>Interview Received: 240<br>Number Enrolled: 150<br>Admitted Rate: 14.8% | Statistics<br>Biochemistry<br>Genetics<br>Systemic Physiology |

| Veterinary School | Avg. GPA & GRE<br><br>Early Decision (ED): Yes/No<br><br>Int'l Students: Yes/No<br><br>Reapps: Yes/No | Admissions Statistics | Science Req. Other than Gen Chem, OChem, Physics, Bio |
|---|---|---|---|
| **Western University**<br><br>309 E. Second St., Pomona, CA 91766 | 3.24 (overall)<br><br>GRE:<br>151 (V)<br>151 (Q)<br><br>ED: N/A<br><br>Int'l Student: Yes<br><br>Reapps: N/A | **(2019)**<br>Apps Received: 935<br>Interview Received: 529<br>Number Enrolled: 105<br>Admitted Rate: 11%<br><br>**(2020)**<br>Apps Received: 935<br>Interview Received: 529<br>Number Enrolled: 105<br>Admitted Rate: 11.2% | Biochemistry w/ Lab<br>Statistics<br>Microbiology<br>Upper Div. Physiology<br>Genetics/Molecular Bio.<br>Upper Div. Bio and Life Sciences<br>Social Sciences |
| **Colorado State Univ.**<br><br>1601 Campus Delivery, Fort Collins, CO 80523 | 3.63 (overall)<br><br>GRE:<br>Not Required<br><br>ED: No<br><br>Int'l Student: Yes<br><br>Reapps: N/A | **(2019)**<br>Apps Received: 2,284<br>Interview Received: N/A<br>Number Enrolled: 149<br>Admitted Rate: 6.5%<br><br>**(2020)**<br>Apps Received: 2,455<br>Interview Received: Not Required<br>Number Enrolled: 150<br>Admitted Rate: 6.1% | Genetics<br>Biochemistry<br>Statistics |
| **Oregon State Univ.**<br><br>700 SW 30th St, Corvallis, OR 97331 | 3.69 (overall)<br>3.66 (science)<br><br>GRE:<br>155 (V)<br>152 (Q)<br><br>ED: No<br><br>Int'l Student: Yes<br><br>Reapps: Yes | **(2019)**<br>Apps Received: 1,118<br>Interview Received: Only for OR residents<br>Number Enrolled: 75<br>Admitted Rate: 6.7%<br><br>**(2020)**<br>Apps Received: 1,197<br>Interview Received: 63 (OR residents)<br>Number Enrolled: 72<br>Admitted Rate: 6.0% | Upper-div Bio.<br>Biochemistry<br>Genetics<br>Math<br>Physiology<br>Statistics |

**WEST**

# VETERINARY PROGRAMS

| Veterinary School | Avg. GPA & GRE<br><br>Early Decision (ED): Yes/No<br><br>Int'l Students: Yes/No<br><br>Reapps: Yes/No | Admissions Statistics | Science Req. Other than Gen Chem, OChem, Physics, Bio |
|---|---|---|---|
| **Washington State**<br><br>100 Grimes Way, Pullman, WA 99164 | 3.67 (overall)<br>3.66 (science)<br><br>GRE:<br>Not Required<br><br>ED: No<br><br>Int'l Student: Yes<br><br>Reapps: Yes | **(2019)**<br>Apps Received: 1,441<br>Interview Received: 395<br>Number Enrolled: 135<br>Admitted Rate: 9.4%<br><br>**(2020)**<br>Apps Received: 1,561<br>Interview Received: 424<br>Number Enrolled: 138<br>Admitted Rate: 8.8% | Genetics<br>Biochemistry<br>Statistics<br>Alg., Pre-calc, or higher |

ALASKA

ARIZONA

CALIFORNIA

COLORADO

HAWAII

IDAHO

MONTANA

NEVADA

NEW MEXICO

OREGON

UTAH

WASHINGTON

WYOMING

# MIDWESTERN UNIVERSITY COLLEGE OF VETERINARY MEDICINE

**Address:** 19555 N 59th Ave., Glendale, AZ 85308
**Website:** *https://www.midwestern.edu/academics/our-colleges/college-of-veterinary-medicine.xml*
**Contact:** *https://online.midwestern.edu/public/reqinfo.cgi*
**Phone:** (630) 515-6171

## COST OF ATTENDANCE

**Tuition:** $67,354
**Fees & Expenses:** $34,517
**Total:** $101,871

**Financial Aid:** https://www.midwestern.edu/admissions/tuition-and-financial-aid/scholarships/scholarships-glendale-campus.xml

## ADDITIONAL INFORMATION

**Interesting tidbit:** The College of Veterinary Medicine offers a two-year pre-clinical and two-year clinical curriculum. The first 8 quarters are a combination of classroom lectures, laboratories, simulation lab exercises. Quarters 9-13 involve diverse clinical rotation training.

**Important Updates due to COVID-19:** Accepts online coursework to fulfill prerequisite requirements. Accepts pass/fail coursework to fulfill prerequisite requirements. Accept online lab coursework.

**Were tests required?** No.

**Are tests expected next year?** No.

**What percent of admitted students participate in international experiences?** N/A

**What percent of current students take an extra year for research or a dual degree?** N/A, Summer Research Fellowship Program and Summer Scholar Program available.

**What service learning opportunities exist?** Shelter Medicine Program: https://www.midwestern.edu/academics/degrees-and-programs/doctor-of-veterinary-medicine-az/shelter-medicine.xml

**NAVLE First-Time Pass Rate:** 96% (year unspecified)

# UNIVERSITY OF ARIZONA COLLEGE OF VETERINARY MEDICINE

**Address:** 1580 E Hanley Blvd., Oro Valley, AZ 85737
**Website:** *https://vetmed.arizona.edu/*
**Contact:** *https://vetmed.arizona.edu/contact*
**Phone:** (520) 621-7048

## COST OF ATTENDANCE

**In-State Tuition:** $47,219
**Fees & Expenses:** $33,573
**Total:** $80,792

**Out-of-State Tuition:** $72,719
**Fees & Expenses:** $33,573
**Total:** $108,293

**Financial Aid:** https://vetmed.arizona.edu/financial-resources

## ADDITIONAL INFORMATION

**Interesting tidbit:** The DVM curriculum at the University of Arizona College of Veterinary Medicine is a three-year, nine-semester, continuous program. During the first six pre-clinical semesters, the curriculum utilizes a hybrid-distributive clinical educational model, through which students are introduced to clinical concepts and skills both in classroom settings and through the use of large and small animals on University property.

**Important Updates due to COVID-19:** The program will accept pass/fail prerequisite courses if taken during Spring and Summer 2020 as part of the COVID-19 consideration. No more than half of a student's prerequisites can be graded pass/fail.

**Were tests required?** No.

**Are tests expected next year?** No.

**What percent of admitted students participate in international experiences?** N/A

**What percent of current students take an extra year for research or a dual degree?** N/A

**What service learning opportunities exist?** N/A

**NAVLE First-Time Pass Rate:** N/A

ALASKA
**ARIZONA**
CALIFORNIA
COLORADO
HAWAII
IDAHO
MONTANA
NEVADA
NEW MEXICO
OREGON
UTAH
WASHINGTON
WYOMING

# WEST

**ALASKA**

**ARIZONA**

**CALIFORNIA**

**COLORADO**

**HAWAII**

**IDAHO**

**MONTANA**

**NEVADA**

**NEW MEXICO**

**OREGON**

**UTAH**

**WASHINGTON**

**WYOMING**

# UC DAVIS SCHOOL OF VETERINARY MEDICINE

**Address:** 1 Garrod Dr., Davis, CA 95616
**Website:** *https://www.vetmed.ucdavis.edu/*
**Contact:** *https://www.vetmed.ucdavis.edu/contact*
**Phone:** (530) 752-1383

## COST OF ATTENDANCE

**In-State Tuition:** $32,161
**Fees & Expenses:** $29,470
**Total:** $61,631

**Out-of-State Tuition:** $44,406
**Fees & Expenses:** $29,470
**Total:** $73,876

**Financial Aid:** https://financialaid.ucdavis.edu/graduate/vet

## ADDITIONAL INFORMATION

**Interesting tidbit:** The University of California, Davis, School of Veterinary Medicine leads the nation in research funding for veterinary schools and colleges and has shaped the field of veterinary medicine, developing dynamic veterinary treatments and making key discoveries related to animals, human and environmental health. As of 2020, the school is ranked No. 1 in the United States by U.S. News & World Report and No. 1 in the world by QS World University Rankings.

**Important Updates due to COVID-19:** Accept credit for prerequisite courses whether taken for a grade or pass/fail only for the spring semester.  The school has always accepted online courses and labs.

**Were tests required?** GRE required.

**Are tests expected next year?** Yes.

**What percent of admitted students participate in international experiences?** N/A, International externships and other opportunities available. For more information, visit: https://www.vetmed.ucdavis.edu/global-programs

**What percent of current students take an extra year for research or a dual degree?** 12.2% dual degree. DVM/MPVM and DVM/PhD available. For more information on these programs, visit: https://vstp.vetmed.ucdavis.edu/

**What service learning opportunities exist?**  Outreach and Public Service available. For more information, visit: https://www.vetmed.ucdavis.edu/outreachpublic-service

**NAVLE First-Time Pass Rate:** 95% (2020)

# WESTERN UNIVERSITY OF HEALTH SCIENCES COLLEGE OF VETERINARY MEDICINE

**Address:** 309 E. Second Street, Pomona CA, 91766
**Website:** *https://www.westernu.edu/veterinary/*
**Contact:** *https://apply.westernu.edu/register/request-information*
**Phone:** (909) 469- 5628

## COST OF ATTENDANCE

**Tuition:** $55,575
**Fees & Expenses:** $21,860
**Total:** $77,435

**Financial Aid:** https://prospective.westernu.edu/veterinary/dvm/tuition-scholarships/

## ADDITIONAL INFORMATION

**Interesting tidbit:** In keeping with the school's reverence-for-life philosophy, animals are not harmed for educational purposes. You will learn anesthesia and surgery through the use of inanimate and dynamic models, computer simulations, and apprenticeships. Cadaver exercises are supplied through WesternU's Willed Deceased Animals for Veterinary Education (WAVE) program.

**Important Updates due to COVID-19:** Accepts online coursework to fulfill prerequisite requirements. Accepts pass/fail coursework to fulfill prerequisite requirements. Accept online lab coursework only for science prerequisites requiring a lab as long as the COVID-19 requires institutions to be closed.

**Were tests required?** GRE or MCAT required.

**Are tests expected next year?** Yes.

**What percent of admitted students participate in international experiences?** N/A, Rotations may be regional, national, or international.

**What percent of current students take an extra year for research or a dual degree?** 4.7% dual degree.

**What service learning opportunities exist?** Veterinary Ambulatory Community Service (VACS) Program.

**NAVLE First-Time Pass Rate:** 92.2% (2019)

ALASKA

ARIZONA

CALIFORNIA

COLORADO

HAWAII

IDAHO

MONTANA

NEVADA

NEW MEXICO

OREGON

UTAH

WASHINGTON

WYOMING

# WEST

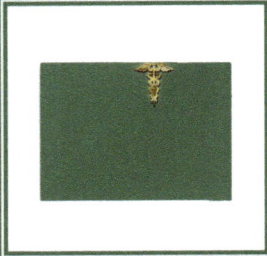

ALASKA

ARIZONA

CALIFORNIA

COLORADO

HAWAII

IDAHO

MONTANA

NEVADA

NEW MEXICO

OREGON

UTAH

WASHINGTON

WYOMING

# COLORADO STATE UNIVERSITY COLLEGE OF VETERINARY MEDICINE AND BIOMEDICAL SCIENCES

**Address:** 1601 Campus Delivery, Fort Collins, CO 80523
**Website:** *https://vetmedbiosci.colostate.edu/dvm/*
**Contact:** *https://vetmedbiosci.colostate.edu/dvm/contact/*
**Phone:** (970) 491-7051

## COST OF ATTENDANCE

**In-State Tuition:** $38,962
**Fees & Expenses:** $16,104
**Total:** $55,066

**Out-of-State Tuition:** $62,660
**Fees & Expenses:** $20,804
**Total:** $83,464

**Financial Aid:** https://vetmedbiosci.colostate.edu/dvm/tuition-and-financial-resources/

## ADDITIONAL INFORMATION

**Interesting tidbit:** The College of Veterinary Medicine and Biomedical Sciences (CVMBS) is made up of four academic departments - Biomedical Sciences, Clinical Sciences, Environmental and Radiological Health Sciences, and Microbiology, Immunology, and Pathology. The college is renowned for programs in infectious disease, oncology, equine surgery and reproduction, and professional communication, among others.

**Important Updates due to COVID-19:** For Spring/Summer/Fall 2020, accept online coursework and pass/fail coursework to fulfill prerequisite requirements and online lab coursework.

**Were tests required?** No.

**Are tests expected next year?** No.

**What percent of admitted students participate in international experiences?** N/A, International learning opportunities available. For more information, visit: https://vetmedbiosci.colostate.edu/dvm/learning-opportunities/

**What percent of current students take an extra year for research or a dual degree?** 33.1% dual degree. For more information on these programs, visit: https://vetmedbiosci.colostate.edu/dvm/special-degree-programs/

**What service learning opportunities exist?** Opportunities. For more information, visit: https://vetmedbiosci.colostate.edu/outside-the-classroom/

**NAVLE First-Time Pass Rate:** 98% (2020)

# OREGON STATE UNIVERSITY COLLEGE OF VETERINARY MEDICINE

**Address:** 700 SW 30th St, Corvallis, OR 97331
**Website:** *https://vetmed.oregonstate.edu/*
**Contact:** *https://vetmed.oregonstate.edu/contacts-directions-and-parking*
**Phone:** (541) 737-2098

## COST OF ATTENDANCE

**In-State Tuition:** $26,688
**Fees & Expenses:** $19,956
**Total:** $46,644

**Out-of-State Tuition:** $51,375
**Fees & Expenses:** $19,956
**Total:** $71,331

**Financial Aid:** https://vetmed.oregonstate.edu/students/future/dvm/financial-matters

## ADDITIONAL INFORMATION

**Interesting tidbit:** Oregon State University is a leader in research and veterinary care of llamas and alpacas with the only endowed professorship in Camelid Medicine and Surgery in the world.

**Important Updates due to COVID-19:** Allow pass/fail coursework from Winter 2020 term through Spring 2021.

**Were tests required?** No.

**Are tests expected next year?** No.

**What percent of admitted students participate in international experiences?** Student-led annual veterinary service trips to locations in Central and South America.

**What percent of current students take an extra year for research or a dual degree?** 1.3% dual degree.

**What service learning opportunities exist?** Partnership with the Oregon Humane Society.

**NAVLE First-Time Pass Rate:** 98% (2020)

ALASKA

ARIZONA

CALIFORNIA

COLORADO

HAWAII

IDAHO

MONTANA

NEVADA

NEW MEXICO

OREGON

UTAH

WASHINGTON

WYOMING

WEST

**ALASKA**

**ARIZONA**

**CALIFORNIA**

**COLORADO**

**HAWAII**

**IDAHO**

**MONTANA**

**NEVADA**

**NEW MEXICO**

**OREGON**

**UTAH**

**WASHINGTON**

**WYOMING**

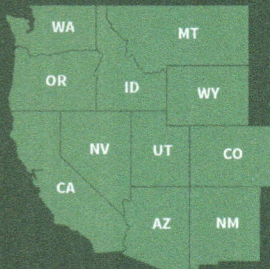

# WASHINGTON STATE UNIVERSITY COLLEGE OF VETERINARY MEDICINE

**Address:** 100 Grimes Way, Pullman, WA 99164
**Website:** *https://www.vetmed.wsu.edu/*
**Contact:** *https://www.vetmed.wsu.edu/Contact-Us*
**Phone:** (509) 335-9515

## COST OF ATTENDANCE

**In-State Tuition:** $26,302
**Fees & Expenses:** $18,746
**Total:** $45,048

**Out-of-State Tuition:** $61,714
**Fees & Expenses:** $18,746
**Total:** $80,460

**Financial Aid:** https://dvm.vetmed.wsu.edu/finances

## ADDITIONAL INFORMATION

**Interesting tidbit:** WSU's College of Veterinary Medicine is home of the WIMU Regional Program in Veterinary Medicine. The WIMU (Washington-Idaho-Montana-Utah) Regional Program is a partnership between the Washington State University College of Veterinary Medicine, University of Idaho Department of Animal and Veterinary Science, Montana State University, and Utah State University School of Veterinary Medicine. Classes are conducted on three campuses (Washington State University, Montana State University, and Utah State University) but the Doctor of Veterinary Medicine (DVM) degree is conferred by the Regents of Washington State University.

**Important Updates due to COVID-19:** Accepts online coursework to fulfill prerequisite requirements. Accepts pass/fail coursework to fulfill prerequisite requirements. Accept online lab coursework.

**Were tests required?** No.

**Are tests expected next year?** No.

**What percent of admitted students participate in international experiences?** N/A. International experiences and courses available. For more information, visit: https://www.vetmed.wsu.edu/academic-programs/international-veterinary-education

**What percent of current students take an extra year for research or a dual degree?** N/A

**What service learning opportunities exist?** For more information on opportunities, visit: https://dvm.vetmed.wsu.edu/Program-Information/opportunities

**NAVLE First-Time Pass Rate:** 94% (2020)

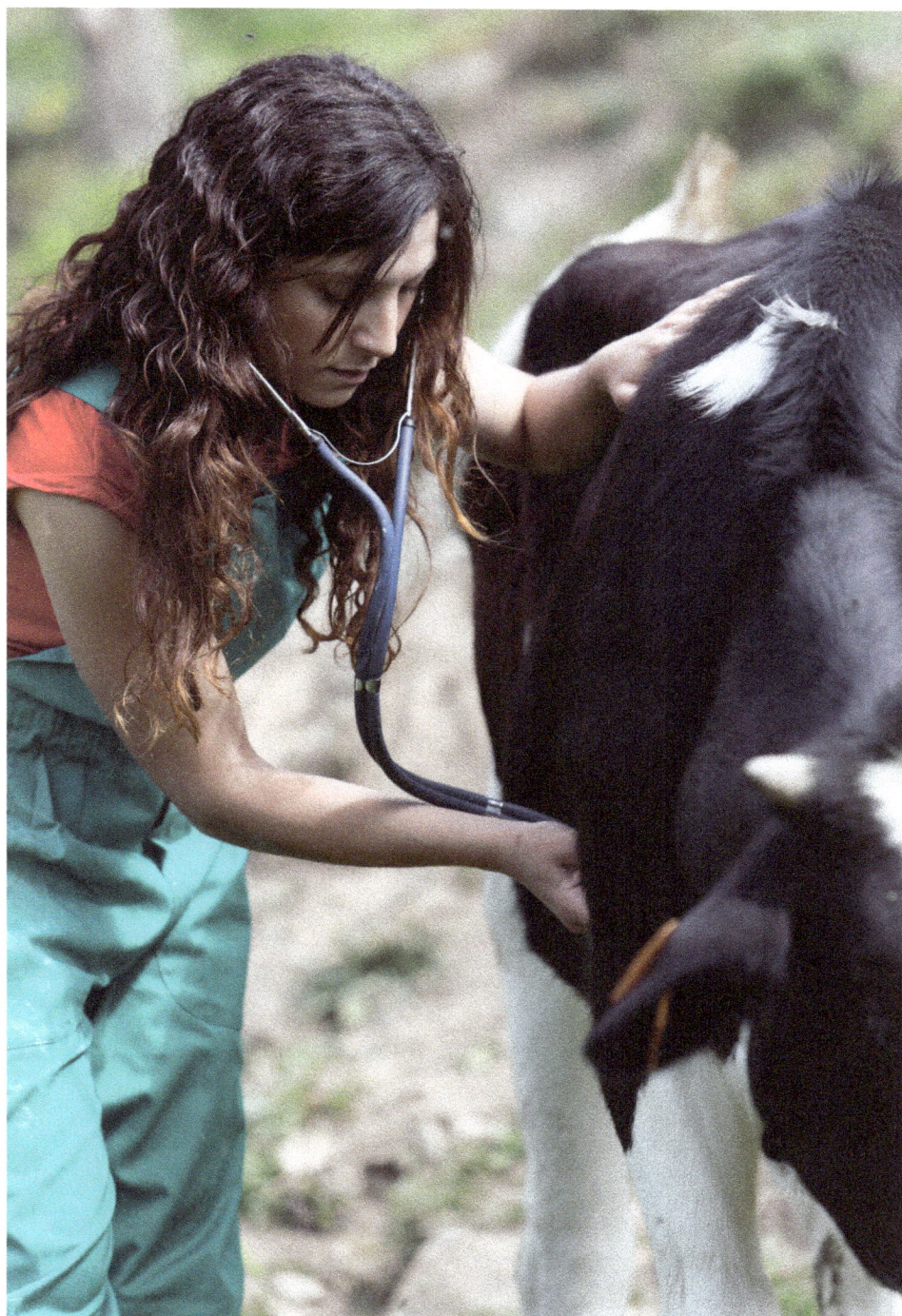

# VETERINARY
# MEDICAL
# SCHOOL LISTS

# CHAPTER 6

# VET SCHOOLS BY CITY/STATE

| Vet Schools | City | State | Region | Website |
|---|---|---|---|---|
| Auburn University College of Veterinary Medicine | Auburn | AL | 3 | https://www.vetmed.auburn.edu/ |
| Tuskegee University School of Veterinary Medicine | Tuskegee | AL | 3 | https://www.tuskegee.edu/programs-courses/colleges-schools/cvm |
| Midwestern University College of Veterinary Medicine | Glendale | AZ | 4 | https://www.midwestern.edu/academics/our-colleges/college-of-veterinary-medicine.xml |
| University of Arizona College of Veterinary Medicine | Oro Valley | AZ | 4 | https://vetmed.arizona.edu/ |
| University of California, Davis School of Veterinary Medicine | Davis | CA | 4 | https://www.vetmed.ucdavis.edu/ |
| Western University of Health Sciences College of Veterinary Medicine | Pomona | CA | 4 | https://www.westernu.edu/veterinary/ |
| Colorado State University College of Veterinary Medicine and Biomedical Sciences | Fort Collins | CO | 4 | https://vetmedbiosci.colostate.edu/dvm/ |
| University of Florida College of Veterinary Medicine | Gainesville | FL | 3 | https://education.vetmed.ufl.edu/ |
| University of Georgia College of Veterinary Medicine | Athens | GA | 3 | https://vet.uga.edu/ |
| Iowa State University College of Veterinary Medicine | Ames | IA | 2 | https://vetmed.iastate.edu/ |
| University of Illinois College of Veterinary Medicine | Urbana | IL | 2 | https://vetmed.illinois.edu/ |
| Purdue University College of Veterinary Medicine | West Lafayette | IN | 2 | https://www.purdue.edu/vet/ |
| Kansas State University College of Veterinary Medicine | Manhattan | KS | 2 | https://www.vet.k-state.edu/ |

| | | | | |
|---|---|---|---|---|
| Louisiana State University School of Veterinary Medicine | Baton Rouge | LA | 3 | https://www.lsu.edu/vetmed/ |
| Tufts University School of Veterinary Medicine | North Grafton | MA | 1 | https://vet.tufts.edu/ |
| Michigan State University College of Veterinary Medicine | East Lansing | MI | 2 | https://cvm.msu.edu/ |
| University of Minnesota College of Veterinary Medicine | St. Paul | MN | 2 | https://vetmed.umn.edu/ |
| University of Missouri - Columbia College of Veterinary Medicine | Columbia | MO | 2 | https://cvm.missouri.edu/ |
| Mississippi State University College of Veterinary Medicine | Mississippi State | MS | 3 | https://www.vetmed.msstate.edu/ |
| North Carolina State University College of Veterinary Medicine | Raleigh | NC | 3 | https://cvm.ncsu.edu/ |
| Cornell University College of Veterinary Medicine | Ithica | NY | 1 | https://www.vet.cornell.edu/ |
| Long Island University School of Veterinary Medicine | Brookville | NY | 1 | https://liu.edu/vetmed |
| Ohio State University College of Veterinary Medicine | Columbus | OH | 2 | https://vet.osu.edu/ |
| Oklahoma State University College of Veterinary Medicine | Stillwater | OK | 3 | https://vetmed.okstate.edu/ |
| Oregon State University College of Veterinary Medicine | Corvallis | OR | 4 | https://vetmed.oregonstate.edu/ |
| University of Pennsylvania School of Veterinary Medicine | Philadelphia | PA | 1 | https://www.vet.upenn.edu/ |
| Lincoln Memorial University College of Veterinary Medicine | Harrogate | TN | 3 | https://www.lmunet.edu/college-of-veterinary-medicine/index.php |
| University of Tennessee College of Veterinary Medicine | Knoxville | TN | 3 | https://vetmed.tennessee.edu/ |

| | | | | |
|---|---|---|---|---|
| Texas A&M University College of Veterinary Medicine & Biomedical Sciences | College Station | TX | 3 | https://vetmed.tamu.edu/ |
| Texas Tech University School of Veterinary Medicine | Amarillo | TX | 3 | https://www.depts.ttu.edu/vetschool/ |
| Virginia Tech Virginia-Maryland College of Veterinary Medicine | Blacksburg | VA | 3 | http://www.vetmed.vt.edu/ |
| Washington State University College of Veterinary Medicine | Pullman | WA | 4 | https://www.vetmed.wsu.edu/ |
| University of Wisconsin-Madison School of Veterinary Medicine | Madison | WI | 2 | https://www.vetmed.wisc.edu/ |

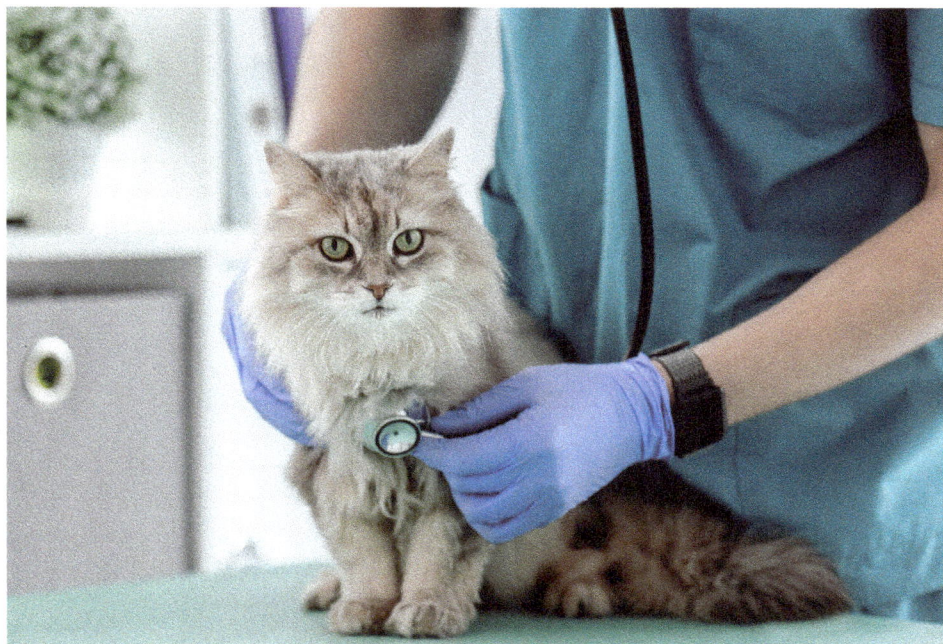

# CHAPTER 7

# VET SCHOOL PREREQUISITES

ALABAMA

| School | Required | Recommended | Notes |
|---|---|---|---|
| Auburn University College of Veterinary Medicine | Written Comp., Literature, Fine Arts, Humanities, History, Social &Behav. Science Electives, Pre-Calc/Trig or higher, Biology w/Lab, Chem. w/Lab, OChemw/Lab, Physics, Cell Biology (see notes), Biochem., Animal Nutrition (see notes), Science Electives (see recommended). | Science electives must include 2+ of the following: comparative anatomy, genetics, embryology, mammalian or animal physiology, microbiology, physics 2, histology, reproductive physiology, parasitology, or immunology | Microbiology or genetics cannot be used to fulfill Cell Biology requirement. Animal nutrition may be taken online. |
| Tuskegee University School of Veterinary Medicine | English or Written Comp., Humanities & Social Studies, Liberal Arts, Math, Medical Terminology, Advanced Biol. Coursework, Biochem. w/Lab, Chem. w/Lab, OChemw/Lab, Physics 1 and 2 w/Labs, Science Electives, Intro to Animal Science, Physical Education (if no B.S. degree). | N/A | No listed information on AP credits. Contact admissions. |

For the number of hours required for prerequisite courses, and for the most up-to-date information, please refer to the individual school websites.

*A.P. credit satisfies the requirement.

** When A.P. credit is awarded, upper-level coursework in the same subject area is required.

*** A.P. credit may satisfy the requirement on a case by case basis

## ARIZONA

| School | Required | Recommended | Notes |
|---|---|---|---|
| Midwestern University College of Veterinary Medicine | Biochem., Biol., Chem. w/Lab, OChemw/Lab, Math (College Algebra or higher), Physics w/Lab, Engl. Comp. Science Electives (see recommended). | Science electives: cell biology, microbio., genetics, animal nutrition, etc. | No listed information on AP credits. Contact admissions. |
| University Of Arizona College of Veterinary Medicine | Biol., Chem., OChem., Physics, Math (Algebra, Trig., Pre-Calc., Calc., or Stats.), English Comp. (writing intensive), Arts & Humanities, and Social Sciences. | Labs not required, but strongly encouraged. | AP credits accepted as long as they are listed on undergraduate transcript.<br><br>Online and community college courses are acceptable.<br><br>No more than half of a student's pre-requisites can be Pass/Fail. |

## CALIFORNIA

| School | Required | Recommended | Notes |
|---|---|---|---|
| University Of California, Davis School of Veterinary Medicine | Physics*, Biol., w/Lab*, Chem. w/Lab*, OChemw/Lab*, Biochem., Genetics, Systemic Physiology, Stats.* | N/A | AP credits accepted as long as they are listed on undergraduate transcript.<br><br>AP credits may fulfill certain courses if applicant receives "3" or higher.<br><br>Official score report from CollegeBoard also required upon admission. |

For the number of hours required for prerequisite courses, and for the most up-to-date information, please refer to the individual school websites.
*A.P. credit satisfies the requirement.
** When A.P. credit is awarded, upper-level coursework in the same subject area is required.
*** A.P. credit may satisfy the requirement on a case by case basis

| School | Required | Recommended | Notes |
|---|---|---|---|
| Western University of Health Sciences College Of Veterinary Medicine | OChemw/Lab, Biochem. or Physiological Chem., Stats., Microbio., Upper Div. Physiology, Genetics or Molecular Bio., Upper Div/ Bio and Life Sciences w/Lab, Humanities/ Social Sciences, Physics w/ Lab, Engl. Comp. | Biochem/ or Physiological Chem. preferably with lab. | AP credits accepted as long as they are listed on undergraduate transcript.<br><br>Virtual labs not accepted.<br><br>Biostatistics may be accepted in lieu of Statistics on case-by-case basis. |

## COLORADO

| School | Required | Recommended | Notes |
|---|---|---|---|
| Colorado State University College of Veterinary Medicine And Biomedical Sciences | Biol. w/Lab, Genetics (see notes), Chem. w/Lab, Biochem. (see notes), Physics, Stats., Engl., Comp., Humanities/ Behavioral & Social Sciences, Electives. | Upper division statistics preferred. | Genetics must have biology as prerequisite.<br><br>Biochem. must have OChem as prerequisite.<br><br>AP English Composition will fulfill prerequisite, not AP English Literature.<br><br>AP credit accepted as long as it is listed on undergraduate transcript. |

For the number of hours required for prerequisite courses, and for the most up-to-date information, please refer to the individual school websites.
*A.P. credit satisfies the requirement.
** When A.P. credit is awarded, upper-level coursework in the same subject area is required.
*** A.P. credit may satisfy the requirement on a case by case basis

## FLORIDA

| School | Required | Recommended | Notes |
|---|---|---|---|
| University of Florida College Of Veterinary Medicine | Biol. w/Lab, Microbio. w/Lab, Genetics, Chem. w/ Lab, OChemw/Lab, Biochem., Physics w/Lab, Stats., Advanced Electives (see recommended), Engl., Humanities & Social Science. | Microbiology intended for Nursing programs will not be accepted.<br><br>9+ credits of Advanced Electives, recommended: Animal Nutrition, Biol. Sciences (Physiology, Human Physiology, Molecular Physiology, Histology, Molecular Biology, Bacterial Pathogens, Parasitology), Advanced Communications, Advanced Psychology, Advanced Business. | AP credits accepted by rules put forth by University of Florida.<br><br>A maximum of 45 credit hours may be granted by combining AICE, AP, CLEP, and IB credit. |

## GEORGIA

| School | Required | Recommended | Notes |
|---|---|---|---|
| University Of Georgia College of Veterinary Medicine | Engl., Humanities or Social Studies, Biol. w/Lab, Chem. w/Lab, OChemw/ Lab, Physics, Biochem., Advanced Biol. Courses (see recommended).<br><br>Online courses not accepted for General Biol., General Chem., Organic Chem., or Physics. | Advanced Biol. recommended: Comparative Anatomy, Physiology, Microbio., Cell Bio. or Genetics. | AP credits accepted as long as they are listed on undergraduate transcript. |

For the number of hours required for prerequisite courses, and for the most up-to-date information, please refer to the individual school websites.
*A.P. credit satisfies the requirement.
** When A.P. credit is awarded, upper-level coursework in the same subject area is required.
*** A.P. credit may satisfy the requirement on a case by case basis

## ILLINOIS

| School | Required | Recommended | Notes |
|---|---|---|---|
| University Of Illinois College of Veterinary Medicine | Biol. w/Lab**, Chem. w/Lab, OChemw/ Lab, Biochem, Physics w/Lab*. | N/A | AP credits accepted as long as they are listed on undergraduate transcript.<br><br>More pre-requisite requirements for individuals applying without an undergraduate degree.<br><br>See admissions for more details. |

## IOWA

| School | Required | Recommended | Notes |
|---|---|---|---|
| Purdue University College of Veterinary Medicine | Chem. w/Lab 1 & 2, OChemw/Lab 1 & 2, Biochem (upper div), Biol. w/Lab 1 & 2, Genetics, Microbio. w/Lab, Physics w/Lab 1 & 2, Stats, Engl. Comp., Communication, Humanities. | Careers in Vet. Medicine (if available) | AP credits accepted as long as they are listed on undergraduate transcript.<br><br>Online lecture courses accepted, however lab courses must be taken in-person. |

For the number of hours required for prerequisite courses, and for the most up-to-date information, please refer to the individual school websites.
*A.P. credit satisfies the requirement.
** When A.P. credit is awarded, upper-level coursework in the same subject area is required.
*** A.P. credit may satisfy the requirement on a case by case basis

## KENSAS

| School | Required | Recommended | Notes |
|---|---|---|---|
| Kansas State University College of Veterinary Medicine | Chem., OChemw/Lab, Biochem., Physics, Biology or Zoology, Microbio. w/Lab, Genetics, Expository Writing, Public Speaking, Social Sciences/Humanities, Electives. | Anatomy and Physiology, Business, Immunology, Animal Sciences. | AP credits accepted as long as they are listed on undergraduate transcript. |

## LOUISIANA

| School | Required | Recommended | Notes |
|---|---|---|---|
| Louisiana State University School of Veterinary Medicine | Biol. w/Lab, Microbio., Chem. w/Lab, OChem, Biochem., College-level Math, Physics, Engl. Comp., Electives. | N/A | AP credit accepted but not used in computation of GPA. Students using AP credits are expected to take higher level university courses. |

## MASSACHUSETTS

| School | Required | Recommended | Notes |
|---|---|---|---|
| Tufts University School of Veterinary Medicine | Bio w/Lab, Chem w/Lab, OChemw/Lab, Physics, Genetics, Biochem, Math, Engl., Social/Behavioral Science, Humanities/Fine Arts. | N/A | AP credits accepted as long as they are listed on undergraduate transcript. |

For the number of hours required for prerequisite courses, and for the most up-to-date information, please refer to the individual school websites.
*A.P. credit satisfies the requirement.
** When A.P. credit is awarded, upper-level coursework in the same subject area is required.
*** A.P. credit may satisfy the requirement on a case by case basis

## MICHIGAN

| School | Required | Recommended | Notes |
|---|---|---|---|
| Michigan State University College of Veterinary Medicine | Math* (College Algebra & Trig. or Pre-Calc or Calc.), Physics w/Lab*, Chem w/Lab*, OChem w/Lab, Biochem., Biology w/Lab*, Upper Level Biol. (see notes) | N/A | Upper Level Biol. includes Cell Biology, Physiology, Neurobiology, Immunology, Genetics, Microbiology, or Histology. |

## MINNESOTA

| School | Required | Recommended | Notes |
|---|---|---|---|
| University of Minnesota College of Veterinary Medicine | Writing, Math (see notes), Stats, General Chem w/Lab, OChem, Biochem, Biology w/Lab, Zoology w/Lab, Genetics, Microbiology w/Lab, Physics, Liberal Education. | N/A | Math: College Algebra, Pre-Calculus, or Calculus. AP credits accepted as long as they are listed on undergraduate transcript. |

For the number of hours required for prerequisite courses, and for the most up-to-date information, please refer to the individual school websites.

*A.P. credit satisfies the requirement.

** When A.P. credit is awarded, upper-level coursework in the same subject area is required.

*** A.P. credit may satisfy the requirement on a case by case basis

## MISSOURI

| School | Required | Recommended | Notes |
|---|---|---|---|
| University of Missouri - Columbia College Of Veterinary Medicine | Composition/Communications, College Algebra/Advanced Math; Biochem, Physics 1 and 2, Biol (see notes), Social Science/Humanistic Studies (see notes). | N/A | Biol: Animal Sciences courses do not qualify towards Biol requirement. Examples of courses to fulfill Biol req. include Genetics, Microbiology, Anatomy, or Physiology. Social Science/Humanistic Studies examples include Economics, History, Political Science, Literature, Mythology, etc. |

## MISSISSIPPI

| School | Required | Recommended | Notes |
|---|---|---|---|
| Mississippi State University College of Veterinary Medicine | Engl. Comp, Speech/Technical Writing, Fundamentals of Public Speaking or junior/senior level technical writing, Humanities/Social Sciences, Math (minimum college alg.), Biol. w/Lab, Microbio. w/Lab, Chem. w/Lab, OChemw/Lab, Biochemistry, Physics, Advanced Science Electives (see recommended). | Advanced science elective examples: animal physiology, histology, immunology, nutrition, zoology, genetics, embryology, etc. | AP credits accepted as long as they are listed on undergraduate transcript. |

For the number of hours required for prerequisite courses, and for the most up-to-date information, please refer to the individual school websites.
*A.P. credit satisfies the requirement.
** When A.P. credit is awarded, upper-level coursework in the same subject area is required.
*** A.P. credit may satisfy the requirement on a case by case basis

## NORTH CAROLINA

| School | Required | Recommended | Notes |
|---|---|---|---|
| North Carolina State University College of Veterinary Medicine | Animal Nutrition, Biochem, Biol. w/Lab, Chem. w/Lab, OChemw/Lab, Genetics, Humanities/Social Sciences, Microbio. w/Lab, Physics w/Lab, Stats., Composition & Writing or Public Speaking or Communications. | N/A | AP credits accepted as long as they are listed on undergraduate transcript. |

## NEW YORK

| School | Required | Recommended | Notes |
|---|---|---|---|
| Cornell University College of Veterinary Medicine | English Comp./Writing (see notes), Biol. w/Lab**, Chem. w/Lab** (see notes), OChem, Advanced Life Science, Biochem., Physics w/Lab*. | Biochem Lab | Engl. req. can be satisfied with GRE V score of 163. AP credits with grade of 4+ are accepted. |
| Long Island University School of Veterinary Medicine | Biol. 1 or Zoology, Biol. 2 or Zoology, Chem. w/Lab, OChem. w/Lab, Biochem., Math or Stats., Genetics, Engl. Comp., and Public Speaking. | Cellular Biol., Sociology, Psych., and Medical Terminology. | No information listed on AP credits. |

For the number of hours required for prerequisite courses, and for the most up-to-date information, please refer to the individual school websites.
*A.P. credit satisfies the requirement.
** When A.P. credit is awarded, upper-level coursework in the same subject area is required.
*** A.P. credit may satisfy the requirement on a case by case basis

## OHIO

| School | Required | Recommended | Notes |
|---|---|---|---|
| The Ohio State University College of Veterinary Medicine | Biochem, Microbiology w/ Lab, Physiology, Communication, Science Electives, Humanities/Social Science Electives. | Communication course should be Public Speaking | AP credits accepted as long as they are listed on undergraduate transcript. |

## OKLAHOMA

| School | Required | Recommended | Notes |
|---|---|---|---|
| Oklahoma State University College of Veterinary Medicine | Engl., Chem. w/ Lab, OChem w/Lab, Biochem., Stats., Physics w/Lab, Animal Nutrition, General Zoology or equivalent w/ Lab, Bio. for Science Majors, Microbiology w/Lab, Genetics, Humanities/Social Sciences, Science and/or Business Elective (see recommended). | Business and commerce courses encouraged. | AP credits accepted as long as they are listed on undergraduate transcript. Nutrition course must cover digestion, absorption, and metabolism. Animal Breeding courses will not cover genetics requirement. Animal Nutrition, Biochemistry, Animal Genetics, and OChem 1 & 2 w/Labs must be taken at a 4-year institution. |

For the number of hours required for prerequisite courses, and for the most up-to-date information, please refer to the individual school websites.
*A.P. credit satisfies the requirement.
** When A.P. credit is awarded, upper-level coursework in the same subject area is required.
*** A.P. credit may satisfy the requirement on a case by case basis

## OREGON

| School | Required | Recommended | Notes |
|---|---|---|---|
| Oregon State University College of Veterinary Medicine | Biol., Upper-Division Biol. w/ Lab, Physics, Chem., w/Lab, OChem, Biochem., Genetics, Math, Physiology, Stats., Engl., Public Speaking, Humanities/Social Sciences. | Additional biochemistry (especially encouraged), additional physiology and/or anatomy, animal reproduction, cell bio., cell physio., epidemiology, histology, immunology, microbio., parasitology, and virology. | AP credits for lower division courses accepted as long as they are listed on undergraduate transcript. |

## PENNSYLVANIA

| School | Required | Recommended | Notes |
|---|---|---|---|
| University Of Pennsylvania School of Veterinary Medicine | Engl., Social Sciences/ Humanities, Physics, Chem., Biol. or Zoology, Microbiology, Biochem, Calc., Stats. | As many science-based courses as possible, especially in Biology.<br><br>Most applicants have minimum 15 semester hours in biology. | AP credits accepted as long as they are listed on undergraduate transcript. |

## TENNESSEE

| School | Required | Recommended | Notes |
|---|---|---|---|
| Lincoln Memorial University College of Veterinary Medicine | Biol. w/Lab, Genetics (Animal Breeding/ Reproduction), Biochem., Adv. Science Electives (upper-level), OChem w/Lab, Chem. w/Lab, Physics, Engl., Social Sciences. | N/A | AP credits accepted as long as they are listed on undergraduate transcript. |

For the number of hours required for prerequisite courses, and for the most up-to-date information, please refer to the individual school websites.
*A.P. credit satisfies the requirement.
** When A.P. credit is awarded, upper-level coursework in the same subject area is required.
*** A.P. credit may satisfy the requirement on a case by case basis

| University Of Tennessee College of Veterinary Medicine | Engl. Comp, Social Sciences/ Humanities, General Biol./Zoology w/Lab, Cellular Biology, Genetics, Chem. w/Lab, OChem w/ Lab, Physics w/Lab, Biochem. | Applicants strongly encouraged to take comparative anatomy, mammalian physiology, and microbiology w/lab. | No mention of AP credits. Contact admissions for information. |

## TEXAS

| School | Required | Recommended | Notes |
|---|---|---|---|
| Texas A&M University College of Veterinary Medicine & Biomedical Sciences | Biol. w/Lab, Microbio. w/Lab, Genetics, Animal Nutrition or Feeds & Feeding, Chem. w/Lab, OChem w/ Lab, Biochem., Stats., Physics w/ Lab, Engl., Speech Communication. | N/A | AP credits accepted as long as they are listed on undergraduate transcript. Applicants must complete 53 hours of pre-requisite coursework by the end of spring semester prior to matriculation.<br><br>In addition, applicants must have completed or be enrolled in OChem 1, Physics 1, and Biochem. 1, prior to Fall Semester of their application. |
| Texas Tech University School of Veterinary Medicine | Animal Nutrition, Biochem., Engl., Bio. w/Lab, Microbio. w/ Lab, Genetics, Chem. w/Lab, OChem. w/ Lab, Stats., and Physics. | N/A | AP credits accepted as long as they are listed on undergraduate transcript. |

For the number of hours required for prerequisite courses, and for the most up-to-date information, please refer to the individual school websites.
*A.P. credit satisfies the requirement.
** When A.P. credit is awarded, upper-level coursework in the same subject area is required.
*** A.P. credit may satisfy the requirement on a case by case basis

## VIRGINIA

| School | Required | Recommended | Notes |
|---|---|---|---|
| Virginia Tech Virginia-Maryland College of Veterinary Medicine | Biol. w/Lab, OChem w/Lab, Physics w/Lab, Biochem., Engl., Math, Humanities/Social Sciences, Medical Terminology. | Suggested elective courses in liberal arts. | AP credits accepted as long as they are listed on undergraduate transcript.<br><br>AP credit for one semester of Engl. will be accepted as long as student takes additional Engl. requirements at a college or university. |

## WASHINGTON

| School | Required | Recommended | Notes |
|---|---|---|---|
| Washington State University College of Veterinary Medicine | Biol. w/Lab, Chem. w/Lab, OChem w/Lab, Genetics, Biochem., Physics w/Lab, Stats., Algebra/Pre-Calc or higher, Engl. Comp/Communications, Arts & Humanities/Social Sciences. | Applicants should take higher level courses even if AP credits satisfy prerequisites. | AP credits accepted.<br><br>Refer to WSU AP Credit Chartfor which courses may be satisfied. If applicant receives bachelor's degree prior to matriculation, then general ed. prerequisites are considered fulfilled regardless of credit hours. |

For the number of hours required for prerequisite courses, and for the most up-to-date information, please refer to the individual school websites.
*A.P. credit satisfies the requirement.
** When A.P. credit is awarded, upper-level coursework in the same subject area is required.
*** A.P. credit may satisfy the requirement on a case by case basis

# WISCONSIN

| School | Required | Recommended | Notes |
|---|---|---|---|
| University of Wisconsin-Madison School of Veterinary Medicine | Biol. or Zoology, Genetics or Animal Breeding; Chem. and Qualitative Chem. w/Lab, OChem., Biochem., Physics, Stats., Engl. Comp. or Journalism, Social Sciences or Humanities. | N/A | AP credits accepted as long as they are listed on undergraduate transcript. |

For the number of hours required for prerequisite courses, and for the most up-to-date information, please refer to the individual school websites.
*A.P. credit satisfies the requirement.
** When A.P. credit is awarded, upper-level coursework in the same subject area is required.
*** A.P. credit may satisfy the requirement on a case by case basis

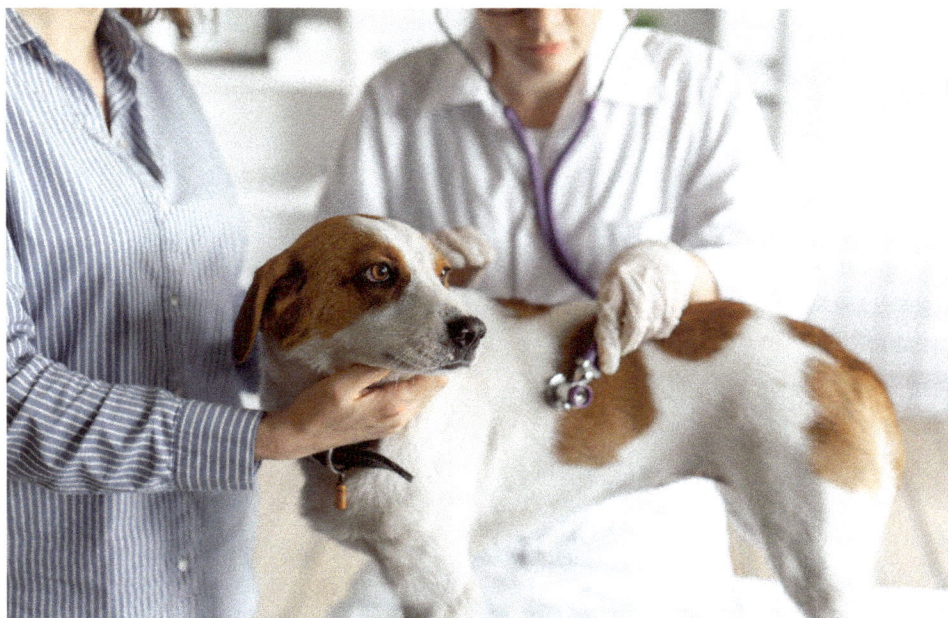

CHAPTER 8

# TOP 10 VETERINARY MEDICAL SCHOOLS

| Ranking | Vet School |
|---------|-----------|
| #1 | University of California, Davis School of Veterinary Medicine |
| #2 | Cornell University College of Veterinary Medicine |
| #3 | Colorado State University College of Veterinary Medicine and Biomedical Sciences |
| #4 | North Carolina State University College of Veterinary Medicine |
| #4 | Ohio State University College of Veterinary Medicine |
| #4 | Texas A&M University College of Veterinary Medicine & Biomedical Sciences |
| #4 | University of Pennsylvania School of Veterinary Medicine |
| #8 | University of Wisconsin-Madison School of Veterinary Medicine |
| #9 | University of Florida College of Veterinary Medicine |
| #10 | University of Georgia College of Veterinary Medicine |

# CHAPTER 9

# VET SCHOOLS BY COST OF ATTENDANCE

| Vet Schools | Tuition (Out-of-State) | COA (Out-of-State) |
|---|---|---|
| Texas Tech University School of Veterinary Medicine | $32,800.00 | $52,590.00 |
| Tuskegee University School of Veterinary Medicine | $41,170.00 | $44,190.00 |
| Texas A&M University College of Veterinary Medicine & Biomedical Sciences | $42,022.00 | $63,582.00 |
| University of California, Davis School of Veterinary Medicine | $44,406.00 | $73,876.00 |
| Purdue University College of Veterinary Medicine | $44,746.00 | $61,556.00 |
| University of Florida College of Veterinary Medicine | $45,500.00 | $65,062.00 |
| Oklahoma State University College of Veterinary Medicine | $46,795.00 | $74,730.00 |
| University of Georgia College of Veterinary Medicine | $47,176.00 | $67,698.00 |
| Michigan State University College of Veterinary Medicine | $47,436.00 | $68,468.00 |
| North Carolina State University College of Veterinary Medicine | $47,657.00 | $67,610.00 |
| Mississippi State University College of Veterinary Medicine | $48,448.00 | $69,418.00 |
| Auburn University College of Veterinary Medicine | $49,040.00 | $72,051.00 |
| Lincoln Memorial University College of Veterinary Medicine | $50,500.00 | $71,614.00 |
| Oregon State University College of Veterinary Medicine | $51,375.00 | $71,331.00 |
| University of Illinois College of Veterinary Medicine | $51,398.00 | $74,364.00 |
| Virginia Tech Virginia-Maryland College of Veterinary Medicine | $51,900.00 | $77,520.00 |
| University of Wisconsin-Madison School of Veterinary Medicine | $52,150.00 | $74,022.00 |
| Louisiana State University School of Veterinary Medicine | $53,227.85 | $82,743.00 |
| Iowa State University College of Veterinary Medicine | $53,304.00 | $136,732.00 |
| Western University of Health Sciences College of Veterinary Medicine | $55,575.00 | $77,435.00 |
| Kansas State University College of Veterinary Medicine | $55,742.00 | $75,470.00 |

| | | |
|---|---|---|
| Long Island University School of Veterinary Medicine | $56,100.00 | $87,597.00 |
| University of Tennessee College of Veterinary Medicine | $56,602.00 | $79,688.00 |
| University of Minnesota College of Veterinary Medicine | $57,948.00 | $76,650.00 |
| Cornell University College of Veterinary Medicine | $58,244.00 | $77,744.00 |
| Tufts University School of Veterinary Medicine | $60,694.00 | $109,858.00 |
| Washington State University College of Veterinary Medicine | $61,714.00 | $80,460.00 |
| Colorado State University College of Veterinary Medicine and Biomedical Sciences | $62,660.00 | $83,464.00 |
| University of Missouri - Columbia College of Veterinary Medicine | $65,170.00 | $86,602.00 |
| Midwestern University College of Veterinary Medicine | $67,354.00 | $101,871.00 |
| University of Pennsylvania School of Veterinary Medicine | $69,278.00 | $94,312.00 |
| University of Arizona College of Veterinary Medicine | $72,719.00 | $106,292.00 |
| Ohio State University College of Veterinary Medicine | $72,923.00 | $95,056.00 |

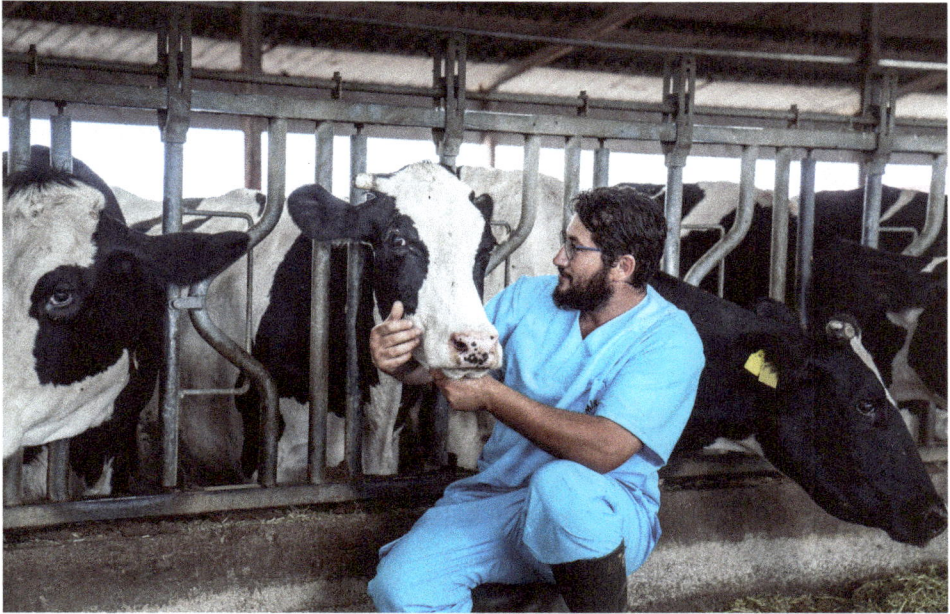

CHAPTER 10

# VET SCHOOLS BY # OF INCOMING STUDENTS

| School | # Enrolled in 2020 |
| --- | --- |
| Tuskegee University School of Veterinary Medicine | 56 |
| Oregon State University College of Veterinary Medicine | 72 |
| Virginia Tech Virginia-Maryland College of Veterinary Medicine | 80 |
| Purdue University College of Veterinary Medicine | 84 |
| University of Tennessee College of Veterinary Medicine | 85 |
| University of Wisconsin-Madison School of Veterinary Medicine | 96 |
| Mississippi State University College of Veterinary Medicine | 97 |
| Long Island University School of Veterinary Medicine | 100 |
| North Carolina State University College of Veterinary Medicine | 100 |
| University of Arizona College of Veterinary Medicine | 100 |
| Tufts University School of Veterinary Medicine | 105 |
| University of Minnesota College of Veterinary Medicine | 105 |
| Western University of Health Sciences College of Veterinary Medicine | 105 |
| Oklahoma State University College of Veterinary Medicine | 106 |
| Louisiana State University School of Veterinary Medicine | 115 |
| Michigan State University College of Veterinary Medicine | 116 |
| Cornell University College of Veterinary Medicine | 120 |
| University of Florida College of Veterinary Medicine | 121 |
| Kansas State University College of Veterinary Medicine | 124 |
| University of Missouri - Columbia College of Veterinary Medicine | 124 |
| Lincoln Memorial University College of Veterinary Medicine | 125 |
| Midwestern University College of Veterinary Medicine | 125 |
| University of Georgia College of Veterinary Medicine | 125 |
| University of Pennsylvania School of Veterinary Medicine | 127 |
| Auburn University College of Veterinary Medicine | 130 |
| University of Illinois College of Veterinary Medicine | 130 |
| Washington State University College of Veterinary Medicine | 138 |
| Colorado State University College of Veterinary Medicine and Biomedical Sciences | 150 |
| University of California, Davis School of Veterinary Medicine | 150 |
| Iowa State University College of Veterinary Medicine | 157 |
| Ohio State University College of Veterinary Medicine | 162 |
| Texas A&M University College of Veterinary Medicine & Biomedical Sciences | 162 |
| Texas Tech University School of Veterinary Medicine | N/A |

# COMPREHENSIVE HEALTH CARE SERIES

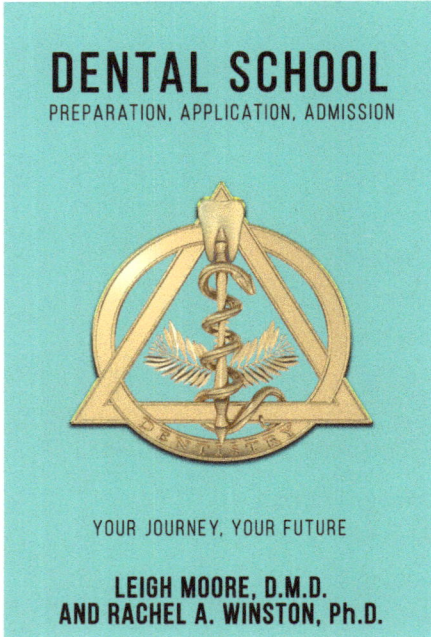

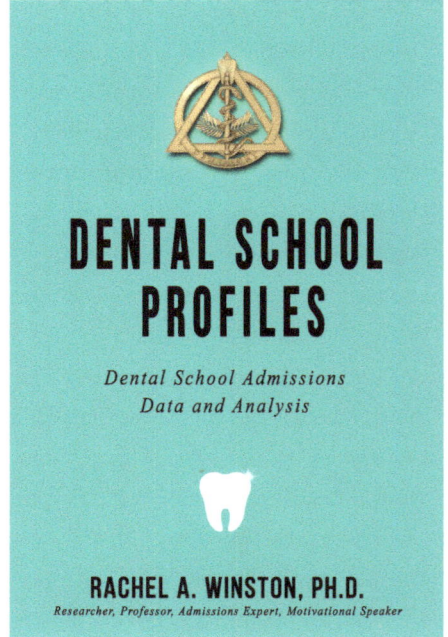

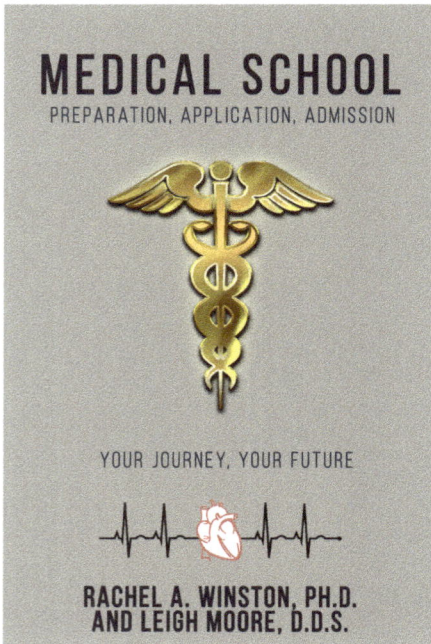

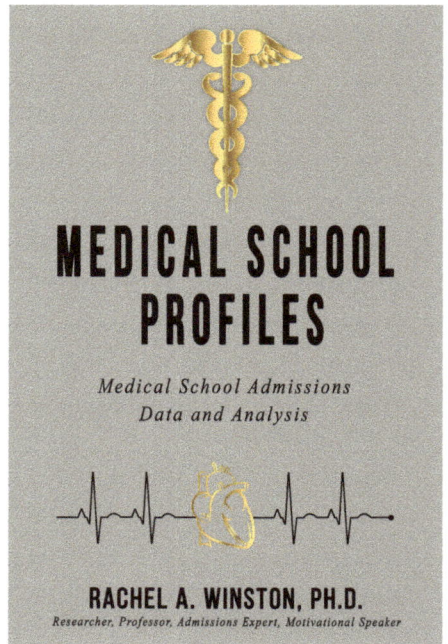

## DENTAL SCHOOL
### PREPARATION, APPLICATION, ADMISSION

YOUR JOURNEY, YOUR FUTURE

**LEIGH MOORE, D.M.D.
AND RACHEL A. WINSTON, Ph.D.**

## DENTAL SCHOOL PROFILES

*Dental School Admissions
Data and Analysis*

**RACHEL A. WINSTON, PH.D.**
*Researcher, Professor, Admissions Expert, Motivational Speaker*

## MEDICAL SCHOOL
### PREPARATION, APPLICATION, ADMISSION

YOUR JOURNEY, YOUR FUTURE

**RACHEL A. WINSTON, PH.D.
AND LEIGH MOORE, D.D.S.**

## MEDICAL SCHOOL PROFILES

*Medical School Admissions
Data and Analysis*

**RACHEL A. WINSTON, PH.D.**
*Researcher, Professor, Admissions Expert, Motivational Speaker*

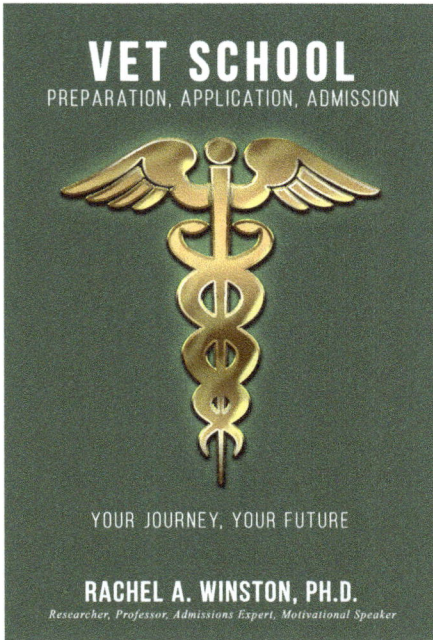

**VET SCHOOL**
PREPARATION, APPLICATION, ADMISSION

YOUR JOURNEY, YOUR FUTURE

RACHEL A. WINSTON, PH.D.
*Researcher, Professor, Admissions Expert, Motivational Speaker*

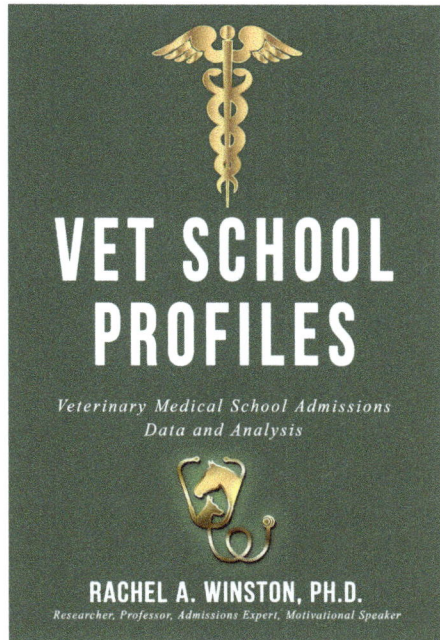

**VET SCHOOL PROFILES**

*Veterinary Medical School Admissions Data and Analysis*

RACHEL A. WINSTON, PH.D.
*Researcher, Professor, Admissions Expert, Motivational Speaker*

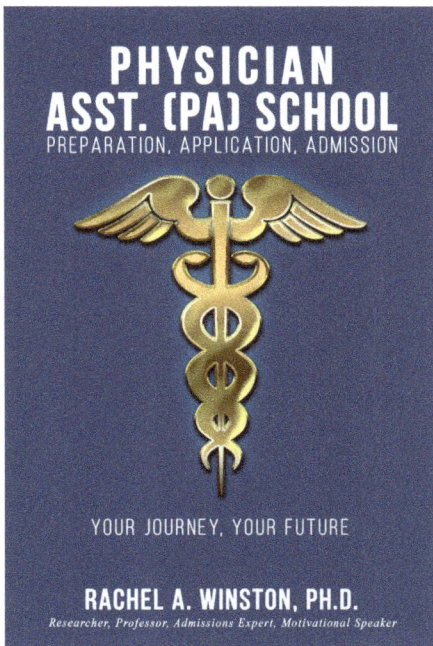

**PHYSICIAN ASST. (PA) SCHOOL**
PREPARATION, APPLICATION, ADMISSION

YOUR JOURNEY, YOUR FUTURE

RACHEL A. WINSTON, PH.D.
*Researcher, Professor, Admissions Expert, Motivational Speaker*

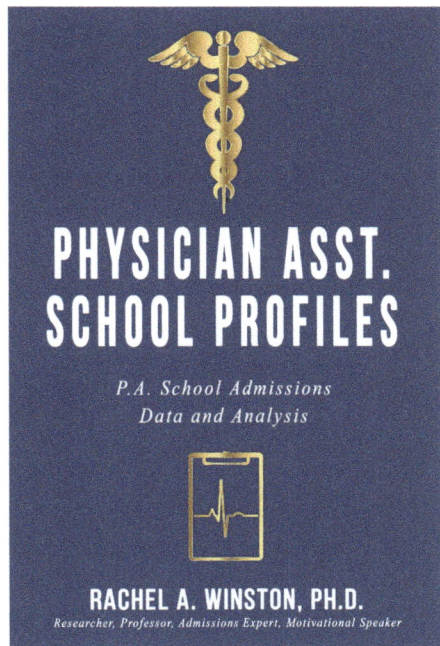

**PHYSICIAN ASST. SCHOOL PROFILES**

*P.A. School Admissions Data and Analysis*

RACHEL A. WINSTON, PH.D.
*Researcher, Professor, Admissions Expert, Motivational Speaker*

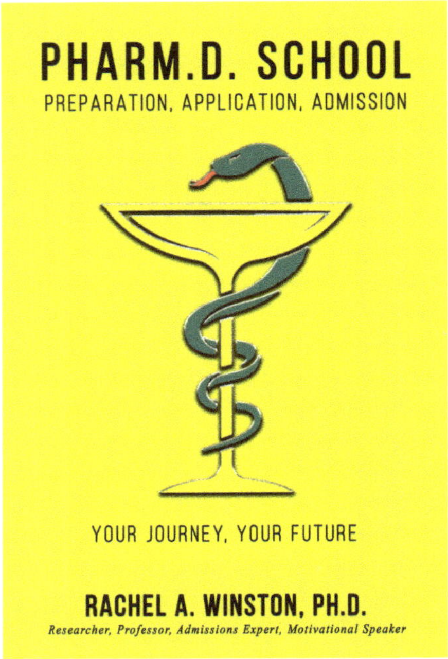

PHARM.D. SCHOOL
PREPARATION, APPLICATION, ADMISSION

YOUR JOURNEY, YOUR FUTURE

RACHEL A. WINSTON, PH.D.
*Researcher, Professor, Admissions Expert, Motivational Speaker*

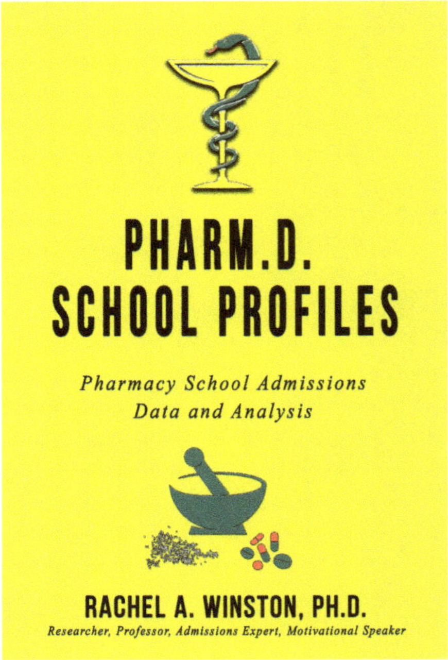

PHARM.D.
SCHOOL PROFILES

*Pharmacy School Admissions
Data and Analysis*

RACHEL A. WINSTON, PH.D.
*Researcher, Professor, Admissions Expert, Motivational Speaker*

OSTEOPATHIC
MEDICAL SCHOOL
PREPARATION, APPLICATION, ADMISSION

YOUR JOURNEY, YOUR FUTURE

RACHEL A. WINSTON, PH.D.
*Researcher, Professor, Admissions Expert, Motivational Speaker*

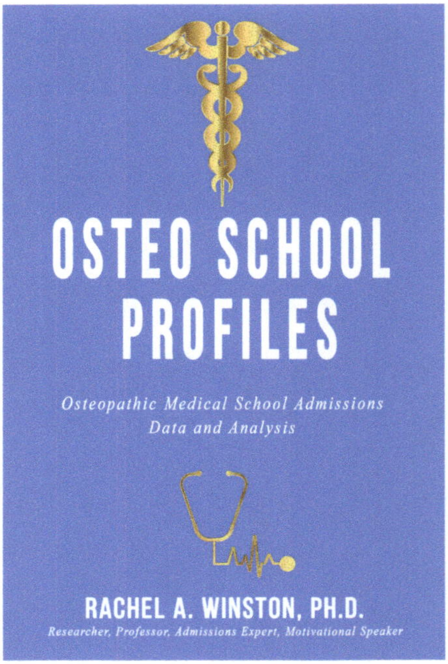

OSTEO SCHOOL
PROFILES

*Osteopathic Medical School Admissions
Data and Analysis*

RACHEL A. WINSTON, PH.D.
*Researcher, Professor, Admissions Expert, Motivational Speaker*

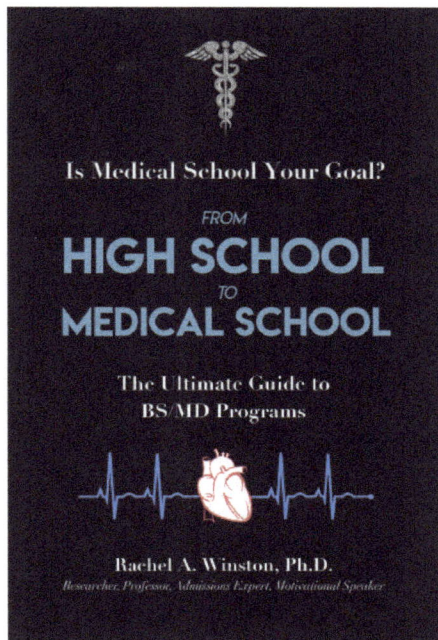

This comprehensive healthcare series is designed in full color to aid the growing number of applicants seeking clear, comprehensive materials. As a college admissions expert and former UCLA College Counseling Certificate Program faculty member, Dr. Winston is dedicated to helping students obtain the information they need.

## FOR MORE INFORMATION

bsmdguide.com

medschoolexpert.com

Purchase books at Lizard-publishing.com

## SERVICES OFFERED BY LIZARD EDUCATION:

- College Counseling
- Admissions News/Resources
- Essay Support and Editing
- Interview Preparation
- Road Trips to Visit Colleges
- Career Planning/Majors/Resumes
- BS/MD, BS/DO, BS/JD, BS/DDS
- Medical School
- Graduate School (Masters & Doctorate)
- Film Studio and Editing

- Portfolio Assistance/SlideRoom
- Athletics Recruiting/Highlight Films
- International Admissions/Visa/TOEFL
- Financial Aid and Scholarships
- UCs, Ivy Leagues, and Colleges Nationwide
- Book Publishing
- Engineering, Robotics, STEM
- Art Portfolios

Email: collegeguide@yahoo.com

Website: collegelizard.com

LIZARD

# INDEX

# O

# P

# T

# U

# V

# W

www.ingramcontent.com/pod-product-compliance
Lightning Source LLC
Chambersburg PA
CBHW052024030426
42335CB00026B/3262